Experience U.S. History!
Activities to Engage ALL Students

Rickey Millwood

Kagan

© 2007 **Kagan Publishing**

This book is published by **Kagan Publishing**. All rights are reserved by **Kagan Publishing**. No part of this publication may be reproduced or transmitted in any form by any means, electronic or mechanical, including photocopy, recording, or any information storage and retrieval system, without prior written permission from **Kagan Publishing**. The blackline masters may be duplicated only by classroom teachers who purchase the book and only for use in their own classrooms. To obtain additional copies of this book, other **Kagan** publications or information regarding professional development, contact **Kagan**.

Kagan Publishing
981 Calle Amanecer
San Clemente, CA 92673
1 (800) 933-2667
Fax: (949) 369-6311
www.KaganOnline.com

ISBN: 978-1-879097-94-0

Introduction
by Rickey Millwood

After teaching history 26 years at Spartanburg High School, I am truly enjoying my teaching more than ever. The students in my classroom are learning more and continue to perform better because their various learning styles are being addressed daily. The reason: I am now teaching with activities and diverse strategies that meet the state standards and engage ALL my students, not just a select few.

I have been a longtime proponent of active learning in the classroom. I have conducted past workshops for the South Carolina State Department of Education that illustrate the importance of integrated curriculum and activities that actively engage all learners. In 2000, I was named the Spartanburg School District 7 Teacher of the Year and participated in the South Carolina Teacher of the Year program. However, in all my years of teaching, nothing has made a greater impact on my instruction than the implementation of multiple intelligence strategies I learned by attending a Kagan workshop.

After the workshop, I began to develop history activities to engage students' eight intelligences:
- Verbal/Linguistic
- Logical/Mathematical
- Visual/Spatial
- Musical/Rhythmic
- Bodily/Kinesthetic
- Naturalist
- Interpersonal
- Intrapersonal

I broadened my activities and had my students make posters, draw cartoons, sing songs, create graphs, and role-play events. Immediately, I enjoyed tremendous success. History became more active and real. Engaging students in meaningful activities greatly enhances student performance and motivation. Students are on task, and they enjoy coming to class. They learn more and their grades are better. My evaluations have been excellent and I credit the Kagan MI strategies I use and share in this book.

Discipline problems have virtually disappeared. Many teachers say discipline is the biggest issue in America, but when a teacher uses Kagan MI strategies and taps into the right intelligences, students become motivated, the learning becomes fun, and there are few discipline issues. There's no doubt about it, using these MI activities improves discipline.

If I have a student in my history class that has a musical intelligence and all I do is lecture, then I do not assist a child in reaching his or her full potential. However, if I have a student who enjoys music, I may have that student write a song on an instrument for the class. Teachers must always be sensitive to all learning styles because we tend to teach how we learn best. Remember to place the student first and move toward meeting his or her learning styles.

By engaging all students in a variety of activities that span the intelligences, all students are more actively engaged. History becomes more experiential. They experience history from the inside, rather than merely hearing and reading about history. Multi modal activities engage students' various intelligences and learning styles and thus they are more interested and retain the information better.

There are 21 chapters in this book, organized sequentially from early America to recent times. For each chapter, there are numerous activity ideas for each of the eight intelligences. Following the activity ideas, are reproducible student pages. The pages have a written summary of a historical event, then either instructions for an activity or activity options for students (or the teacher). Collectively, there are nearly 2,000 activity ideas. To do each activity would be impossible. Simply, pick and choose the ones you feel are most pertinent to your class and content.

My greatest success in teaching history is to do two to three activities per day. Each day, I address different intelligences with different activities. Students approach the subject matter through a range of intelligences, reinforcing the historical concepts and facts. Agreed, this is an unconventional approach to teaching history, but my observations and test scores suggest that the state standards can be more than met while teaching the content through activities that address various learning styles.

By instructing through activities that involve all learners, students stay on task and produce a much higher quality of work. They become excited about the class and perform up to their full potential. I have seen a major improvement in attitude and enthusiasm in my classes. It's most rewarding to hear students say that history is their favorite class and they look forward to attending class each day.

Use these Kagan MI activities and your students will want to come to class because they enjoy the learning through engaging and experiential activities. I'm confident you'll find plenty of great ideas and activities to use in this book as you and your students experience U.S. history!

Acknowledgements

- Miguel Kagan — Concept and Development
- Erin Kant — Illustration
- Jennifer Duke — Graphic Design
- Becky Herrington — Publications Manager
- Alex Core — Cover Layout and Color
- Kimberly Fields — Copyediting

U.S. History Standards
Through Multiple Intelligence Activities

The key to effective teaching and learning involves bringing all students into the lesson every day. Teachers must decide the most effective means of instructional approach to address the state standards daily and yet meet all students' needs. History standards can be addressed and met through activities that involve the multiple intelligences. Using diverse teaching strategies will make the lessons more interesting and challenging for the students. This book provides the classroom teacher with hundreds of student-based activities from the time of Early Colonies to the present-day conflict in Iraq.

U.S. History Standards Addressed in this Workbook

- ★ Early Colonization and Major Colonial Events
- ★ The Revolutionary War and the Formation of the U.S. Constitution
- ★ Judicial Review and Historical Supreme Court Decisions
- ★ The Age of Thomas Jefferson
- ★ Manifest Destiny and Social Reforms
- ★ President Jackson's Democracy
- ★ Popular Sovereignty
- ★ Slavery and the Causes of the Civil War
- ★ The Civil War and Reconstruction
- ★ Native Americans and the Western Frontier
- ★ The Gilded Age and the Great Labor Strikes
- ★ Foreign Affairs and the Great War
- ★ The Roaring '20s
- ★ The Great Depression and the New Deal
- ★ World War II and the Holocaust
- ★ The Events of the Cold War
- ★ America's Conflicts in Asia
- ★ Civil Rights
- ★ Détente and the Fall of Communism
- ★ Desert Storm and the Fight Against Terrorism
- ★ New Challenges in the Middle East

Table of Contents

Chapter 1—Life and Events in Early America (1565-1763) 6

Chapter 2—A Call for Revolution and Government (1763-1790) 14

Chapter 3—Jefferson's Democracy to the Era of Good Feelings (1800-1824) 22

Chapter 4—The Era of Jackson (1824-1844) 30

Chapter 5—Expansion and Reform (1835-1869) 38

Chapter 6—The Peculiar Institution and the Causes of The Civil War (1840-1865) 46

Chapter 7—The Civil War and Reconstruction (1861-1877) 54

Chapter 8—The American West (1865-1900) 62

Chapter 9—The Gilded Age (1877-1900) 70

Chapter 10—The Progressive Movement and Foreign Affairs (1900-1918) 78

Chapter 11—The Era of World War I (1914-1919) 86

Chapter 12—The Roaring '20s (1920-1929) 94

Chapter 13—The Great Depression (1929-1942) 102

Chapter 14—Roosevelt's New Deal (1932-1945) 110

Chapter 15—World War II and the Holocaust (1939-1945) 118

Chapter 16—Living Through the Early Cold War Years (1945-1969) 126

Chapter 17—A Time for Civil Rights (1954-1970) 134

Chapter 18—The Era of Vietnam (1954-1975) 142

Chapter 19—Détente and Life Through the '70s (1968-1980) 150

Chapter 20—The Conclusion of the Cold War and New Challenges (1990-2000) 158

Chapter 21—Recent Events in Our Nation's History (2001-2005) 166

Experience U.S. History! • Rickey Millwood
Kagan Publishing • 1 (800) 933-2667 • www.KaganOnline.com

Chapter 1
Life and Events in Early America
(1565-1763)

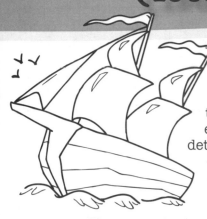

The story of America's growth began with the first permanent settlement in St. Augustine, Florida, by the Spanish. Soon, the English settled the new land and the Thirteen Colonies emerged. The early Colonies developed and thrived through the determination and courage of the first settlers. Despite facing many obstacles, the settlers developed a prosperous region along the Atlantic seaboard.

⭐ Verbal/Linguistic ⭐

1 Compare and contrast the Spanish Colonies with the English Colonies.

2 Write an essay about the founding of St. Augustine or Jamestown.

3 Complete a creative writing exercise about Nathaniel Bacon's Rebellion in Virginia.

4 Write a story about the causes of the Great Awakening.

5 Write a newspaper article about the banishment of Roger Williams.

6 Write a speech by Anne Hutchinson, stating her religious beliefs.

7 Read *The Crucible*.

8 Read about the implications of the Peter Zenger case.

9 Explain to a partner the concept of *mercantilism*.

10 Read *The Scarlet Letter*.

11 Read about, then write a paper on, the brutality of Barbados slave codes.

12 Write a letter as if you lived in Puritan New England during the Salem Witch Trials.

⭐ Logical/Mathematical ⭐

1 Analyze data that contributed to the early problems confronted in Jamestown.

2 Classify and categorize the major tools needed by the settlers of Jamestown.

3 List and organize facts about the Puritan Colonies.

4 Synthesize ideas about Bacon's Rebellion.

5 Calculate the number of free men, slaves, and women in the early Colonies from 1607 to 1725.

6 Make a graph that shows what happened to the Native American population between 1607 and 1763.

7 Calculate the average life span of an early settler in the Colonies.

8 Make a log of trends of treatment toward Native Americans by the Colonists.

9 Estimate the economic damage done by King Philip's War.

10 Graph trends in the various immigrant groups that settled the first American Colonies.

Experience U.S. History! • Rickey Millwood
Kagan Publishing • 1 (800) 933-2667 • www.KaganOnline.com

 ## Visual/Spatial

1 Design a postcard of Puritan New England.

2 Draw a political cartoon about the Salem Witch Hunts.

3 Draw a scene from King Philip's War.

4 Make a poster about one of the original Thirteen Colonies.

5 Create a PowerPoint of the Thirteen Colonies and illustrate their major crops.

6 Create a map that indicates the location of Native American groups before 1607.

7 Create an advertisement for indentured servants in Europe.

8 Design a book cover about an event in Colonial America.

9 Build a model of a stockade fort.

10 Design clothing worn by the early settlers.

11 Design a sculpture of a character from Colonial America.

12 Build a model of the *Mayflower*.

Musical/Rhythmic

1 Identify the major instruments played in Colonial America.

2 Compare and contrast Native American musical instruments with European instruments.

3 Compose a song about a major event in Colonial America.

4 Research several songs of the Colonial era and determine the theme.

5 Evaluate the influence that European music had upon the early Colonies.

6 Identify the type of music performed by slaves in the Southern Colonies.

7 Sing a song from the Colonial period to the class.

8 Compare and contrast church music of the Southern and New England Colonies.

9 Build an instrument like those from Colonial America.

Chapter 1 continued
Life and Events in Early America
(1565-1763)

 Bodily/Kinesthetic

1 Role-play Anne Hutchinson as she was banished by the Puritans.

2 Perform a skit about a major event in Colonial America.

3 Visit a historical town such as Williamsburg, Jamestown, Charleston, Savannah, or St. Augustine.

4 Role-play Jonathon Edwards as he begins the Great Awakening.

5 Use kitchen utensils similar to those found in Colonial America.

6 Prepare foods eaten during the Colonial period.

7 Re-enact the signing of the Mayflower Compact.

8 Dress as people from Colonial America.

9 Create a layout of an early Colonial city.

10 Perform a play about the first Thanksgiving.

 Naturalist

1 Describe the terrain and topography of Jamestown.

2 Examine regions in South Carolina where rice plantations were located.

3 Record changes in the soil after tobacco was planted in the Middle Colonies.

4 List the physical characteristics of America before Europeans arrived.

5 Categorize the animals in America before the Europeans arrived.

6 Identify the foods grown by Native Americans before St. Augustine was settled by the Spanish.

7 Record the developmental stages of the Thirteen Colonies.

8 Use the Internet to research artifacts from a Colonial museum.

9 Tour a fort in a historical town such as St. Augustine, Florida.

10 Research how the early explorers used stars to chart a course to America.

11 Describe how the terrain of America changed during the first 100 years after Jamestown was settled.

Experience U.S. History! • Rickey Millwood
Kagan Publishing • 1 (800) 933-2667 • www.KaganOnline.com

Interpersonal

1 Debate the effects of Bacon's Rebellion on the aristocracy in the Colonies.

2 Discuss in groups the treatment of Native Americans by Colonists.

3 Discuss with a partner the banishment of Roger Williams to Rhode Island.

4 Do a team presentation on the Barbados Slave Code.

5 Discuss Stono's Rebellion and determine its consequences.

6 Share with others the importance of growing tobacco in the early Colonies.

7 Interview each other about the causes of King Philip's War.

8 As a team, show pictures of weapons used by the Native Americans and the Colonists.

9 Plan an event about Colonial America.

10 Solve problems as a team that the early Colonists faced in early Virginia.

Intrapersonal

1 Prioritize items the Colonists would have needed for survival upon the arrival at Jamestown.

2 Do a reflective writing activity, describing how the Wampanoag were affected after the arrival of the Europeans.

3 Write about the actions to banish Roger Williams.

4 Using a graphic organizer weigh alternatives to using slaves on rice plantations in South Carolina.

5 Describe your feelings about the Salem Witch Trials in a poem.

6 Write about mood changes in Charleston, South Carolina, after Stono's Rebellion.

7 Reflect upon the actions of George Whitfield as he spread the Great Awakening. Share your thoughts with a friend.

8 Describe the feelings of Ben Franklin after he heard George Whitfield speak.

9 Express your likes and dislikes about the treatment of women in Colonial America.

10 Defend the position by Britain to make Georgia a buffer colony.

11 Write an ethical code of conduct the Colonists could have followed concerning the treatment of slaves and Native Americans.

12 Defend the Native American position to fight for their way of life and culture.

Experience U.S. History! • **Rickey Millwood**
Kagan Publishing • 1 (800) 933-2667 • www.KaganOnline.com

1.1 Blackline Master • Interpersonal Activity

Life and Events in Early America

Early Jamestown

In 1607, the first permanent English Colony was established at Jamestown, Virginia. However, the settlers selected a terrible location for their fort—a swampy region infested with mosquitoes. The new settlers soon faced some serious problems such as malaria, cold weather, starvation, and attacks from Native Americans. Most of the early settlers perished, but through sheer determination and courage, some survived until assistance arrived a year later. One major reason the colonists had such a difficult time was because some believed hard work was beneath their dignity. This was soon rectified by John Smith who believed that if one did not work, then one would not receive food. Early Jamestown settlers managed to survive despite extreme hardships.

Instructions: As a pair, discuss and write solutions to the following four problems the Colonists faced in 1607.

A. Disease. _____
_____
_____
_____

B. Native American attacks. _____
_____
_____
_____

C. Weather. _____
_____
_____
_____

D. Starvation. _____
_____
_____
_____

Life and Events in Early America

Witch Hunts in America

Imagine hearing women scream they were completely innocent of the crime of witchcraft. Such was the scene in Puritan New England. In 1692, innocent women were put to death in Salem, Massachusetts. A scary movement had fallen over Massachusetts. This started because of bazaar behavior observed in two young women. Perhaps sick with some type of illness, these girls showed symptoms considered to be associated with witchcraft.

According to Cotton Mather, hysterical behavior could only be caused by the devil, and those showing erratic behavior were witches. Before the hysteria ended, over 300 people in New England would be charged with witchcraft and 24 would perish. This wild search for witches among society would last a full year.

In 1950, Senator Joe McCarthy from Wisconsin accused large numbers of Americans of being Communists. He even intimidated the president through his rough and daring tactics. In his mind, America was full of dangerous Communists just as Salem was full of witches. Finally, in 1954, these wild and unfounded accusations came to an end. As a result of these episodes, the term *Witch Hunt* is synonymous with being unfairly blamed or unjustly accused.

In fall 2005, Congress blamed FEMA for not responding to Hurricane Katrina victims fast enough. FEMA officials stated that Congress was on a Witch Hunt and they were unjustly blamed for the lingering disaster in New Orleans.

Activity Options

 Role-play and conduct a trial of women accused of witchcraft in Salem.

 Did Federal Emergency Management Agency officials react correctly to the circumstances in Louisiana, or did Congress search for a scapegoat? Simulate a press conference where FEMA officials defend their actions.

1.3 B... ...aster • Naturalist Activity

Life and Events in Early America

Economies of the Early Middle Colonies

The early Colonies were divided into three distinctive regions. Each region made a separate, but crucial contribution to our nation's early economy. These regions included New England, the Middle Colonies, and the South. Each of these regions had an economy dependent upon the natural environment. The economy of New England relied upon heavy timber that could be used for construction. New England also had good harbors and an abundance of fish off the coast. The economies of the Middle and Southern Colonies depended upon the soil and climate. These two regions produced lucrative cash crops. The terrain and climate were the two major factors that determined what could be produced in each region.

Instructions: Create a map of the Colonies that identifies the major crops or products each region produced.

1.4 Blackline Master • Logical/Mathematical Activities

Life and Events in Early America

The Slave Trade and Immigration

In 1619, Dutch slave ship arrived in the Colonies. Slavery would begin in Colonial America and would not end until the conclusion of the Civil War. Large numbers of Native Americans had been enslaved but had perished as a result of disease. Another source of labor was needed on a large scale to grow the cash crops that reaped huge profits.

Early slaves were used on plantations in the deep South to grow rice and tobacco. Imagine being placed in the sweltering heat of South Carolina and forced to grow rice in malaria-infested water. These were the conditions the slaves were forced to endure.

Soon, these slaves would fall under extremely brutal rules, which came to be known as the Barbados Slave Codes.

These slaves played a major role in the development of the early Middle and Southern Colonies. They performed the labor that produced food and crops for the Colonies. They also brought their rich African culture. Other groups, such as the French, Welch, Germans, and Scots, would later come to Colonial America. However, it was the Africans that made up the second largest group of immigrants in the early Colonies.

Activity Options

1. Identify patterns of different ethnic groups who settled in the Colonies.

2. List and organize facts about different ethnic groups that settled the Colonies.

3. Discover trends in Europe that encouraged immigration to the American Colonies.

4. Locate the regions in the Colonies where most slaves were located.

5. Make predictions about early slave revolts in the Colonies.

Experience U.S. History! • Rickey Millwood
Kagan Publishing • 1 (800) 933-2667 • www.KaganOnline.com

Chapter 2

A Call for Revolution and Government (1763–1790)

Competition over resources and territorial expansion led France and Great Britain into war in America. The close of the French and Indian War then brought a rift between the Colonies and the British. The Proclamation of 1763 was just the beginning of the many causes that led to the American Revolutionary War. Dramatic events, such as the Boston Massacre and Boston Tea Party, would follow. The new nation was ready to declare its Declaration of Independence and form its own Constitution.

★ Verbal/Linguistic ★

1 Discuss the causes of the French and Indian War.

2 Discuss the Proclamation of 1763.

3 Write a newspaper article about the Boston Massacre.

4 Read the Declaration of Independence.

5 Explain how the Northwest Ordinance of 1785 influenced public education.

6 Give a speech that protests the Sugar Act or Stamp Act.

7 Make a word web about the Parliamentary Acts forced upon the Colonies.

8 Write a report on Samuel Adams, Richard Henry Lee, or Patrick Henry.

9 Share ideas about the role of African Americans in the Revolutionary War.

10 Explain the differences between Tories and Patriots.

11 Discuss the Articles of Confederation and point out the major weaknesses.

12 Read primary sources about life in America during the Revolutionary War.

13 Read about George Washington's famous crossing of the Delaware River.

★ Logical/Mathematical ★

1 Analyze data about the advantages the British had going into the Revolutionary War.

2 Brainstorm ideas that demonstrate how the Colonists defeated the British.

3 Compare and contrast the views of the Patriots and Tories.

4 Calculate the probability that the Colonies would win their freedom, based on supplies going into the conflict.

5 List or organize facts about the Native Americans once the Revolutionary War began.

6 Make a graphic organizer about the causes that led to the Revolutionary War.

7 Compare and contrast American soldiers' and British soldiers' diets.

8 Synthesize ideas that explain why the French entered on the side of the Americans.

9 Make associations from the movie *The Patriot* with Francis Marion.

10 Analyze data about Washington's days at Valley Forge in winter 1777.

11 Brainstorm ideas discussed at the First Continental Congress.

Experience U.S. History! • Rickey Millwood
Kagan Publishing • 1 (800) 933-2667 • www.KaganOnline.com

Visual/Spatial

1 Design a postcard about one major American event previous to the Revolutionary War.

2 Make a poster about one major British person during the Revolutionary War.

3 Sketch an event that you feel led to the Revolutionary War.

4 Design a brochure about the Stamp Act.

5 Make a PowerPoint of five major events of the Revolutionary War era.

6 View on the Internet a Revolutionary War battlefield.

7 Create a crossword puzzle about major American persons in the Revolutionary War.

8 Draw a political cartoon about the Boston Massacre.

9 Draw a scene of the Boston Tea Party.

10 Create a political cartoon about the Intolerable Acts.

11 Watch the film called *The Patriot*.

12 Sketch a scene of the British surrender at Yorktown.

Musical/Rhythmic

1 Compose a melody about the Revolutionary War.

2 Play an instrument for the class that was played during the Revolutionary era.

3 Identify any patriotic songs from the Revolutionary War.

4 Identify which musicals instruments were used in battle during the Revolutionary War.

5 Write a jingle about the Boston Tea Party.

6 Perform a patriotic song as a duo for the class.

7 Interpret the lyrics to "Yankee Doodle."

8 Compare and contrast American and British music from the Revolutionary period.

9 Identify several American song writers during the Revolutionary War.

10 Listen to the song "Swamp Fox" about Francis Marion.

Chapter 2 continued

A Call for Revolution and Government
(1763-1790)

Bodily/Kinesthetic

1 Perform a skit about the Boston Tea Party.

2 Act out the role of King George III after shots were fired at Lexington and Concord.

3 Role-play the delegates at the Second Continental Congress.

4 Visit a Revolutionary War battlefield.

5 Act out the role of a Colonial family in Georgia after hearing war had broken out.

6 Perform a skit about the British surrender at Yorktown.

7 Perform a pantomime, illustrating an American victory in the Revolutionary War.

8 Ten students role-play the Bill of Rights for the class. Each student represents a different amendment.

9 Role-play Alexander Hamilton arguing for the creation of a National Bank.

10 Role-play Thomas Jefferson arguing against a National Bank.

Naturalist

1 Label on a map the major engagements of the Revolutionary War.

2 Observe the site of the Boston Massacre on the Internet.

3 Visit historical Philadelphia or Boston.

4 Describe the topography of South Carolina where Francis Marion led his campaign against the British.

5 Research the weather conditions General Washington faced at Valley Forge in 1777.

6 Find and interpret the painting *George Washington Crossing the Delaware*.

7 Bring foods to class that the Continental Army ate during the American Revolution.

8 Record changes to the land in America due to the Revolutionary War.

9 Identify the types of wood used to construct ships during the Revolutionary period.

10 Visit in person or on the Internet a Colonial plantation such as Walnut Grove, South Carolina.

11 Categorize the weapons used in the Revolutionary War.

12 Discuss the color of uniforms in the Revolutionary War.

Experience U.S. History! • Rickey Millwood
Kagan Publishing • 1 (800) 933-2667 • www.KaganOnline.com

Interpersonal

1 Discuss with a partner the weakness of the Articles of Confederation.

2 Debate the decision to locate the nation's capital in Washington DC.

3 Interview each other about Washington's presidency.

4 Discuss with a partner how Washington handled the Whiskey Rebellion.

5 Share with others five major causes of the Revolutionary War.

6 Take the role of a Tory family in Georgia and argue against the war.

7 Do group presentations about American generals during the war.

8 Reach a consensus on why three branches of government were outlined in the U.S. Constitution.

9 Write a paper on the role of Abigail Adams during the Revolutionary War.

10 Discuss with a partner why George Washington agreed to free slaves that supported the Colonial Army.

11 Debate the issue of the Three-Fifths Compromise at the end of the war.

12 Do a team presentation that details U.S. policy toward Native Americans after 1789.

13 Compare and contrast the American and French Revolutions.

14 Discuss with a partner the differences between the Federalists and Anti-Federalists.

15 Share with others your thoughts about the selection of Washington as the first U.S. president.

Intrapersonal

1 Prioritize items needed by soldiers in the Revolutionary War.

2 Using a graphic organizer, record mood changes in Washington's men during the winter of 1777 at Valley Forge.

3 Observe the change in General Washington after his first victory at Christmas. Share your findings with a partner.

4 Defend the position by the French to intervene in the war after the Battle of Saratoga.

5 Describe the feelings the French held toward the British after the conclusion of the French and Indian War.

6 Form an action plan by the Continental Congress after the first shots of the war were fired.

7 Explain in writing the mood changes in Colonial America after the Stamp Act.

8 Write about the actions of Crispus Attucks in the Boston Massacre.

9 Write about the actions of John Adams to defend the British officers that fired shots during the Boston Massacre.

10 Weigh alternatives to the Three-Fifths Compromise.

11 Express your likes and dislikes about the effects of the Boston Tea Party.

12 Write about the four recommendations from President Washington as he left from the presidency.

Experience U.S. History! • Rickey Millwood
Kagan Publishing • 1 (800) 933-2667 • www.KaganOnline.com

2.1 Blackline Master • Musical/Rhythmic Activity

A Call for Revolution and Government

Songs of War

In fact, American history is full of songs that have inspired our nation in troubled times. These songs are nationalistic and arouse our patriotism. Even our attitudes and moods can be reflected through the songs we listen to each day. Songs were played in Colonial times to inspire our nation in its struggle against the mighty British Empire.

Today, we hear many patriotic songs about the conflicts in Afghanistan and Iraq, but time could change that. Songs tend to be patriotic when war first breaks out but can quickly change. Causalities and the length of a war can have a major impact or the tone of songs. The conflict in Vietnam is a classic example of how songs changed. That conflict certainly demonstrated how a nation can turn against a war. This was evident through an avalanche of protest music in the late 1960s.

Instructions: Write a song about the role that American women played in the Revolutionary War.

2.2 Blackline Master • Visual/Spatial Activity

A Call for Revolution and Government

The Boston Massacre

A rowdy crowd in Boston began to throw snowballs laced with rocks at British soldiers in Boston. A bloody result quickly followed.

In March 1770, a group of citizens in Boston, who, resented seeing British soldiers, began to intimidate and harass these men. The soldiers had been sent to control mobs and protect British officials who collected custom fees. Citizens of Boston began to taunt these soldiers. The British soldiers were so frightened and angry that they shot into the crowd and killed five citizens. One of the first to die was Crispus Attucks.

The British soldiers were arrested and placed on trial but were represented by John Adams, who would later become our second president. The British officer Thomas Preston and most of his men were acquitted. Two of the British soldiers were found guilty of the lesser charge of manslaughter and were dismissed from the army.

Instructions: Imagine you were an illustrator at the scene of the Boston Massacre. Draw a picture that captures the event.

Experience U.S. History! • Rickey Millwood
Kagan Publishing • 1 (800) 933-2667 • www.KaganOnline.com

A Call for Revolution and Government

The Boston Tea Party

On December 16, 1773, a group of the Sons of Liberty disguised themselves as Native Americans. Their intent was to board British ships and dump tea into Boston Harbor. Over 300 chests of tea were tossed into the harbor to protest the British Parliament's right to collect a tax on tea.

The protest dealt with the right to collect a tax on tea—not the price of the tea. Citizens in Boston had mixed views about this act of vandalism. This action resulted in drastic measures toward the city of Boston in the form of the Intolerable Acts.

Instructions: Defend or condemn the decision to toss the tea into Boston Harbor as a means of protest.

2.4 Blackline Master • Logical/Mathematical Activity

A Call for Revolution and Government

The Revolutionary War

The chances of the American Colonies being able to defeat the mighty British Empire at the beginning of the war looked bleak. How could the Colonies possibly break away with overwhelming odds against them?

The British had a powerful navy to blockade the ports. The Colonies would not be able to sell any products nor receive any goods. The British would also try to bring in slaves and Native Americans against the Colonies. To make matters worse, the Colonies were divided among themselves between Patriots and Tories.

Since most revolutions fail without foreign intervention, success for the Americans did not appear likely when the first shots were fired. It is truly a miracle that the Colonists defeated the strongest nation in the world.

Instructions: Compare and contrast soldiers in the Revolutionary War.

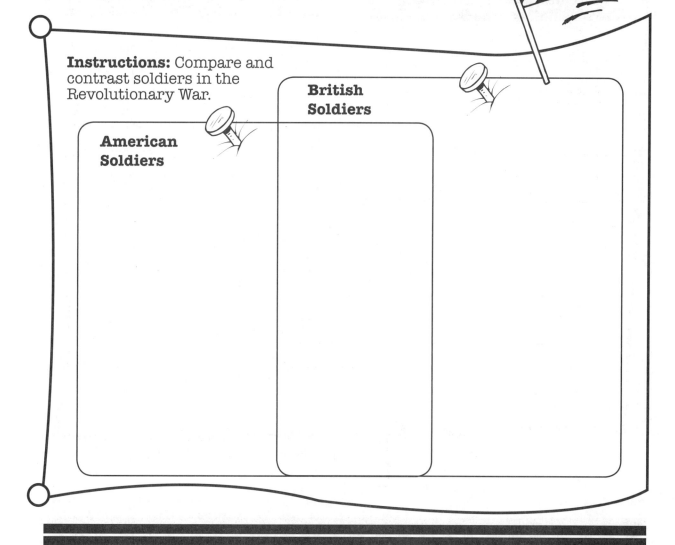

Chapter 3: Jefferson's Democracy to the Era of Good Feelings (1800-1824)

The acquisition of the Louisiana Territory through a purchase by the administration of Thomas Jefferson ranks as one of the most important events in all of American history. Expecting to purchase New Orleans from Napoleon Bonaparte, American diplomats grabbed up the entire middle section of America for a bargain price. The nation instantly expanded its territory but still faced many economic and political challenges. Politically, the British were still rivals in America. President Madison would lead the second fight against the British. President Monroe led the nation into the period called the Era of Good Feelings.

Verbal/Linguistic

1. Discuss the concept of Jeffersonian Democracy.

2. Give a speech supporting the purchase of the Louisiana Territory.

3. Create a slogan about the Louisiana Purchase.

4. Compare and contrast the Revolutionary War with the War of 1812.

5. Explain why the War of 1812 is called Mr. Madison's War.

6. Write a persuasive paper supporting the Monroe Doctrine.

7. Discuss the implications from the *Marbury v. Madison* case.

8. Discuss the impact the Lewis and Clark expedition had upon Native Americans.

9. Write a newspaper article about Thomas Jefferson's views on slavery.

10. Write about the Monroe Doctrine using descriptive language.

11. Share ideas about Henry Clay's Great American System.

Logical/Mathematical

1. Determine the area that makes up the Louisiana Purchase.

2. List and prioritize reasons why the purchase of the Louisiana Territory was important to the United States.

3. Estimate the number of Native Americans that lived in the Louisiana Territory.

4. Predict how the purchase of the Louisiana Territory would expand slavery.

5. Calculate the amount per acre paid for the Louisiana Territory.

6. List and organize facts about the Lewis and Clark Expedition.

7. Evaluate the cost in American lives in the War of 1812.

8. List and organize facts about the Sioux.

9. Make predictions about what happened to Native Americans that lived in the Louisiana Territory.

10. Estimate the cost of building a system of roads such as Henry Clay proposed.

★ Visual/Spatial ★

1 Chart the route of Lewis and Clark.

2 Draw a map of the Louisiana Purchase.

3 Create a crossword puzzle about the Louisiana Purchase.

4 Design a flier, urging men to accompany Lewis and Clark to the Pacific.

5 Create a political cartoon, depicting Andy Jackson as the hero of the Battle of New Orleans.

6 Create a postcard about the Era of Good Feelings.

7 Draw a political cartoon about the Monroe Doctrine.

8 Create a newspaper article and political cartoon, from the British point of view, about the Monroe Doctrine.

9 Draw a political cartoon about the Monroe Doctrine.

10 Make a poster, detailing the provisions of the Missouri Compromise.

★ Musical/Rhythmic ★

1 Listen to the song "Battle of New Orleans" by Johnny Horton.

2 Interpret the song lyrics of "Battle of New Orleans."

3 Play the "Battle of New Orleans" on musical instruments for the class.

4 Listen to the words of the "Star-Spangled Banner," which was written during the battle at Fort McHenry.

5 Determine how musical instruments changed in America from the Colonial period to 1816.

6 Identify the instruments played by Native Americans in the region of Indiana and Ohio.

7 Evaluate the music and songs performed by African Americans on Southern plantations.

8 Write a jingle about a new product invented around 1825.

9 Discover several love ballads from the Age of Jefferson. Share the lyrics of one song with a friend.

Experience U.S. History! • Rickey Millwood
Kagan Publishing • 1 (800) 933-2667 • www.KaganOnline.com

Chapter 3 continued
Jefferson's Democracy to the Era of Good Feelings (1800–1824)

Bodily/Kinesthetic

1 Act out the role of John Marshall in a historical Supreme Court case.

2 Act out the role of Thomas Jefferson in an attempt to expand the United States westward.

3 Perform a skit about Lewis and Clark.

4 Classify the animals spotted on the Western plains by Lewis and Clark.

5 Use physical gestures between Lewis and Clark toward the Native Americans they encountered.

6 Act out the role of James Madison after the War of 1812 breaks out.

7 Build a model of a cotton gin and discuss its impact on American history.

8 Perform a skit about Andy Jackson's victory at New Orleans.

9 Act out the role of a newspaper writer covering the military campaign of Andy Jackson.

10 Role-play James Monroe as he proclaims his Monroe Doctrine.

Naturalist

1 Observe (through the Internet) the phenomena that Lewis and Clark saw as they crossed the Rockies.

2 Observe the changes on a U.S. map as a result of the Louisiana Purchase.

3 Classify the physical features of the Rockies.

4 Categorize the vegetation found in the Louisiana Territory.

5 Record the changes in American settlements after the Louisiana Territory opened.

6 Travel the trail that Lewis and Clark took on their way to the Pacific.

7 Visit a national park located in the region of the Louisiana Territory.

8 Record any changes in American Indian Territory after the Battle of Tippecanoe.

9 Observe and record changes in farming techniques as settlements advanced westward.

10 List the characteristics of the land now called the Dakotas.

11 Visit the location where Lewis and Clark first spotted the Pacific Ocean.

12 Classify the foods and livestock now produced in the central part of the United States.

13 Record the changes in the soil that Lewis and Clark would have observed as they traveled from Missouri to Oregon.

14 Visit Pikes Peak, named in honor of explorer Zebulon Pike.

Experience U.S. History! • Rickey Millwood
Kagan Publishing • 1 (800) 933-2667 • www.KaganOnline.com

Interpersonal

1 Discuss the decision by Napoleon Bonaparte to sell the Louisiana Territory to the United States.

2 Discuss with a partner the causes of the War of 1812.

3 In small groups formulate a plan that would have prevented the War of 1812.

4 Do a team presentation on how the Battle of New Orleans made Andy Jackson a national hero.

5 Write a collaborative essay explaining why the presidency of James Monroe is called the Era of Good Feelings.

6 Think about the actions of President Monroe as he proclaimed the Monroe Doctrine.

7 Weigh alternatives to the Monroe Doctrine.

8 Take a stance in support of the Monroe Doctrine.

9 Take turns stating the major accomplishments of Jefferson, Madison, and Monroe.

10 Do a team presentation about the life of Dolle Madison.

11 Debate why the Federalists detested Mr. Madison's War.

12 Share with others your opinion of the Hartford Conference.

Intrapersonal

1 Make a list of President Jefferson's top priorities.

2 Make an action plan to prevent Washington DC from being burned in the War of 1812.

3 Weigh alternatives to the expansion of slavery across the deep South.

4 Describe your feelings about Madison's presidency.

5 Express in writing the mood changes in New England as a result of the War of 1812.

6 Defend the purpose of the Monroe Doctrine.

7 Describe the changes in European nations as a result of the Monroe Doctrine.

8 Express your feelings about the invention and rapid development of the cotton gin.

9 In a diary, record your feelings about westward expansion through American Indian Territory.

10 Write an ethical code of conduct the Americans should have implemented toward the Native Americans as they passed through their territory.

11 Express your likes and dislikes about Henry Clay's Great American System.

12 Take a stance against the Missouri Compromise.

3.1 Blackline Master • Intrapersonal Activity

Jefferson's Democracy to the Era of Good Feelings

The Louisiana Purchase

During the Jefferson administration, the United States made one of the greatest purchases in its history. In 1803, the United States purchased the Louisiana Territory from Napoleon Bonaparte of France. This acquisition, which gave our nation a section of land that stretched from New Orleans all the way to Canada, provided America an opportunity to grow.

This purchase was made for the bargain price of only $15 million. Napoleon was desperate for money as a result of his European wars, so he decided to sell—a huge block of territory. Thomas Jefferson was prepared to offer France $10 million for just New Orleans. However, much to the shock of American diplomats, France accepted a $15 million offer for the entire territory. The United States had made this great purchase for only pennies per acre!

Instructions: Make an action plan to send an expedition to explore this new territory.

☐ _____
☐ _____
☐ _____
☐ _____
☐ _____
☐ _____
☐ _____
☐ _____
☐ _____
☐ _____
☐ _____
☐ _____
☐ _____

Jefferson's Democracy to the Era of Good Feelings

The War of 1812

In 1812, the United States and Britain would go to war for a second time. A major issue that caused the war was impressment. American sailors were being forced into the British service and navy. The United States regarded this action as highly illegal—a form of piracy. Also, there was great concern that the British were behind the Native American uprisings.

The war hawks in Congress intended to teach the British a lesson. This conflict became known as Mr. Madison's War. The British burned Washington DC but the Americans were able to hold their own.

In New Orleans, Louisiana, Andy Jackson defeated the British. This victory made Andy Jackson a national hero. This was especially unpopular in New England and the first talk of secession was heard there. This region was suffering economic devastation because of the war. After the American victory, those Federalist, calling for secession at the Hartford Convention were seen as unpatriotic. This pretty much finished off that political party. America had proved a second time, it could hold its own against an old rival and world power.

Instructions: Using descriptive language, explain the impact of the burning of Washington DC in our nation's history.

3.3 Blackline Master • Bodily/Kinesthetic Activities

Jefferson's Democracy to the Era of Good Feelings

The Great American System

We have all heard the slogan, "All Roads lead to Rome". America had a politician that was an advocate of a road system to connect the major cities. Henry Clay of Kentucky was truly one of America's greatest politicians and planners. Known as the Great Compromiser, Clay is perhaps our nation's most popular politician that never became president.

Senator Clay believed that growth and prosperity in America would take place if three elements were in place. He favored road construction, tariffs, and a bank—the Great American System. The public supported his plan for better roads, but Congress still felt it was the job of the states to carry out the construction. Tariffs were raised to generate revenue but were disliked in Southern states. The nation had a National Bank until Andy Jackson, an opponent of Clay, destroyed it.

During the Eisenhower administration of the 1950s, the Interstate Highway Act was passed. This project would carry out the vision of Henry Clay. Interstate roads would connect every major U.S. city. This highway system would make it possible to move people and materials quickly in case of emergencies.

Activity Options

1. Role-play both Henry Clay and President Dwight Eisenhower and present an argument on the need for massive road construction in America.

2. Design a model of the United States in 1820 that shows Henry Clay's vision of roads through the nation.

3. Role-play President Madison and create his argument against the federal government's involvement in road construction.

3.4 Blackline Master • Naturalist Activities

Jefferson's Democracy to the Era of Good Feelings

The Missouri Compromise

The Great Compromiser, Henry Clay, gave the nation a reprieve from Civil War for nearly 40 years through his Missouri Compromise. The nation had expanded immensely due to the purchase of the Louisiana Territory. However, there were two major problems to be considered about new states. One problem dealt with the balance of power in the Senate and the other was the issue of slavery.

In 1820, Maine and Missouri were ready to come into the nation as new states. Would they enter as slave or free states? Would the Senate be in favor of the free states?

George Washington had warned of sectionalism, and that's exactly what was tearing at the heart of the nation. To avoid a shift in power and preserve the nation, Henry Clay offered the Missouri Compromise. Maine would enter the nation as a free state, and Missouri would come in as a slave state. Slavery would become illegal north of 36°30'N. For a time, the nation would remain intact. The Great Compromiser had put war on hold.

Activity Options

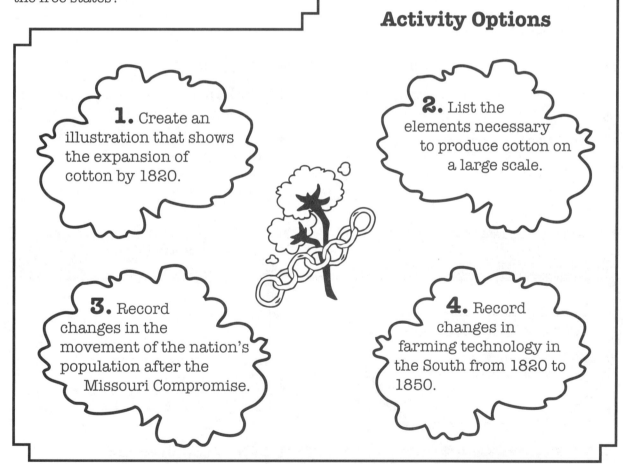

1. Create an illustration that shows the expansion of cotton by 1820.

2. List the elements necessary to produce cotton on a large scale.

3. Record changes in the movement of the nation's population after the Missouri Compromise.

4. Record changes in farming technology in the South from 1820 to 1850.

Experience U.S. History! • **Rickey Millwood**
Kagan Publishing • 1 (800) 933-2667 • www.KaganOnline.com

Chapter 4: The Era of Jackson (1824-1844)

Following an earlier disputed election, the Jackson administration filled American history with many memorable events. The expansion into Texas, which drew America into conflict with Mexico, and the removal of the Five Civilized Tribes were both major events of the period. Andy Jackson was the common man's president; he personally took charge and shaped the events of his administration. This period is also marked by the beginning of tension between the North and South over tariffs and slavery.

⭐ Verbal/Linguistic ⭐

1 Discuss how voting patterns changed in America after 1824.

2 Create a slogan about the outcome of the 1824 presidential election.

3 Write a paper about the Corrupt Bargain.

4 Create a joke about the Spoils System.

5 Share ideas about Andy Jackson's interpretation of the presidency.

6 Discuss Andy Jackson's opposition to the National Bank.

7 Compare and contrast the policies of the Whigs and Democrats of this period.

8 Complete a creative writing exercise about Jackson's inauguration.

9 Tell a tall tale about Davy Crockett, America's first celebrity.

10 Write a persuasive paper arguing for the abolition of slavery.

11 Read about the history and impact of Robert Fulton's steam engine.

12 Write a research paper on the advancement of America's transportation system.

⭐ Logical/Mathematical ⭐

1 Graph the outcome of the 1824 election.

2 Graph the increase in voters between the 1824 and 1828 elections or the increase in voters from 1824 to 1844.

3 Estimate the length of the Trail of Tears.

4 Estimate the number of Native Americans that died along the Trail of Tears.

5 Analyze data about the removal of the Five Civilized Tribes.

7 Make predictions about Jackson's destruction of the National Bank.

9 Calculate the probability that Specie Circular would be successful.

10 List and organize facts about the bitterness that existed between Henry Clay and Andy Jackson.

11 Graph the affect the Panic of 1837 had upon the American economy.

13 Make associations among Andy Jackson, Davy Crockett, and William Henry Harrison.

14 Synthesize ideas about the Denmark Vesey uprising.

16 Describe the contributions of Dorothea Dix.

Visual/Spatial

1 Interpret a political cartoon of Andy Jackson dressed as a king.

2 Create a political cartoon about the declared independence of Texas.

3 Interpret a painting of the Trail of Tears.

4 Draw a political cartoon about the Indian Removal Act.

5 Imagine you heard rumors about the Peggy Eaton affair. Draw a picture for a gossip magazine and write the caption.

6 Create a PowerPoint about Denmark Vesey and his slave uprising.

7 Design a brochure for the 1828 election.

8 Design a political cartoon condemning the Spoils System.

9 Draw a scene about the work of Dorothea Dix.

10 Create a time line of the major events of Jackson's presidency.

11 Create a scene about canal construction.

12 Create a PowerPoint about the steam engine and river boats.

Musical/Rhythmic

1 Listen and interpret the lyrics to the song "Indian Reservation" by the band Paul Revere & the Raiders.

2 Interpret the lyrics of "Dugello" and then listen to the Ballad of the Alamo.

3 Note any changes in musical instruments from 1824 to 1844.

4 Write a song about the Trail of Tears.

5 Compare and contrast music in the North and South during the 1840s.

6 Write about any major changes in music from the 17th century to 18th century.

7 Perform as a team a dance from the early 1800s.

8 Listen with sensitivity to the religious songs of slaves on Southern plantations.

9 Identify any songs about the Underground Railroad.

10 Listen and interpret the lyrics of the song "Erie Canal."

11 Write a song about any event during the Era of Jackson.

Chapter 4 continued
The Era of Jackson
(1824-1844)

Bodily/Kinesthetic

1 Act out the role of Henry Clay and John Quincy Adams in the Corrupt Bargain.

2 Act out the role of Andy Jackson when he won the presidency in 1828.

3 Act out the role of Davy Crockett defending Native American rights in Congress.

4 Perform a skit about the Underground Railroad.

5 Perform a skit about the Trail of Tears.

6 Build a model of a log cabin, similar to the one paraded around by William Henry Harrison in the 1840 campaign.

7 Visit the path taken by the Cherokee as they were removed to Oklahoma.

8 Simulate about the hardships along the Trail of Tears.

9 Perform a skit about Jackson's determination to end the National Bank.

10 Role-play John C. Calhoun when he stepped down from the Jackson administration.

Naturalist

1 Visit the home of Andy Jackson in Nashville, Tennessee.

2 Visit the birthplace of Davy Crockett near Johnson City, Tennessee.

3 Visit the Cherokee Reservation in Cherokee, North Carolina.

4 Attend the play *Unto These Hills*, which depicts the history of the Cherokee in North Carolina.

5 Follow the Trail of Tears.

6 List the characteristics of Oklahoma where the Five Civilized Tribes were relocated.

7 Record changes in the Native American population due to Jackson's policies.

8 Visit the regions where the Choctaw, Chickasaw, Creek, Cherokee, and Seminole reside.

9 Visit the battlefields of Fallen Timbers and Tippecanoe.

10 Visit the Alamo in San Antonio, Texas.

Experience U.S. History! • Rickey Millwood
Kagan Publishing • 1 (800) 933-2667 • www.KaganOnline.com

Interpersonal

1 Discuss in pairs the consequences of the Corrupt Bargain.

2 Role-play the scene of Andy Jackson and his supporters after losing the 1824 election.

3 Interview each other about the Indian Removal Act and the Trail of Tears.

4 Share with others your opinion of the removal of the five tribes that were relocated to Oklahoma.

5 Write a collaborative paper about the impact of the Peggy Eaton Affair.

6 Solve the problem of the Panic of 1837, caused by Jackson's financial policies.

7 Reach a consensus on the outcome of the Indian Removal Act.

8 Mediate the conflict over the Nullification Crisis.

9 Discuss with a partner Jackson's view of the Spoils System.

10 Debate the issue of rotation of servants in office after serving one term.

11 Interview each other about how America changed during the Jackson administration.

12 Criticize the financial policies of Andy Jackson.

Intrapersonal

1 Describe your feelings about the Indian Removal Act.

2 Observe the changes in the mood of Americans toward Native Americans after the discovery of gold in Georgia. Express your thoughts in a poem.

3 Make an action plan that would have solved the Nullification Crisis.

4 Make an action plan that would have prevented Jackson from destroying the National Bank.

5 Reflect on and write about this period of American history.

6 Write about the major needs of the nation by 1840.

7 Using a graphic organizer weigh Jackson's alternatives to the Peggy Eaton Affair without losing a vice president.

8 Write an ethical code of conduct that should have been carried out through the Indian Removal Act.

9 Think about the actions of the American government in charging the Cherokee $6 million to be removed to Oklahoma. Share your thoughts with a partner.

10 Defend the position by Henry Clay as he presented his Great American System.

11 Mediate over the effect of the closing of the National Bank.

12 Describe your feelings about the Underground Railroad.

The Era of Jackson

President Jackson and the National Bank

It's difficult to imagine the United States without the Federal Reserve System. But, our nation was left without a National Bank after President Jackson decided not to renew the charter. Remember that Alexander Hamilton promoted the bank but it was removed during the Jackson administration.

President Andy Jackson was an opponent to the National Bank as he felt it served the purpose of only the wealthy in New England. He believed this bank was not in the best interest of the common man. Jackson objected to the operational procedures of the bank and referred to it as a "hydra of corruption." Jackson launched and destroyed the bank in a two-prong attack. He withdrew federal deposits and did not renew the charter.

Instructions: Create a political cartoon of Jackson's belief that the National Bank was unconstitutional.

The Era of Jackson

The Indian Removal Act

Being relocated and forced to walk hundreds of miles while watching family members die on a trail of misery to Oklahoma was the fate of the Cherokee people. These were the same people that had helped Andy Jackson in the Creek Uprising. This brutal event remains a terrible stain upon the nation's history. The discovery of gold and the greedy desire for land caused an act to be passed that would greatly affect the Native Americans—the Indian Removal Act. This act allowed for the removal of the Choctaw, Chickasaw, Creek, Seminole, and Cherokee to the Oklahoma territory.

The Cherokee were forced on a death march known as the Trail of Tears. In 1838, about 25 percent of the Cherokees died before making it to Oklahoma. Today, this scene is re-created each summer in the outdoor drama *Unto These Hills*.

Instructions: Describe your feelings about the Indian Removal Act.

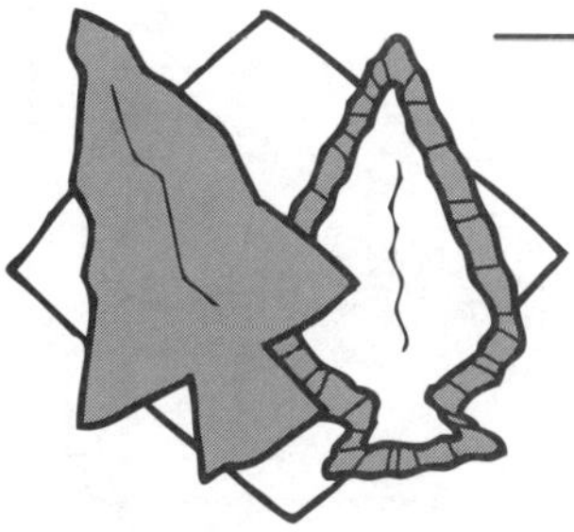

___

___

___

___

___

___

___

___

___

___

___

___

___

___

The Era of Jackson

The Impact of Eli Whitney's Cotton Gin

Inventions in history have both positive and negative consequences, and the cotton gin was no exception. This machine could clean the seeds out of cotton 50 times faster than a human. But the cotton gin had a dramatic impact upon the nation—it increased or fostered slavery. Plantation owners now had an invention that would allow them to expand into the deep South toward Texas. Slaves could plant and pick more cotton while the gin cleaned it. Cotton from these plantations could now feed the industrial North.

Slavery expanded into Texas. This changed the balance of power in Congress because Texas came into the Union as a slave state. Whitney's patent was infringed upon by Southern planters; he made little money from his invention. The cotton gin played a role in leading to the Civil War.

Instructions: Write a letter, as an abolitionist, to Eli Whitney condemning his invention.

_____
_____
_____
_____
_____
_____
_____
_____
_____
_____
_____
_____

4.4 Blackline Master • Logical/Mathematical Activity

The Era of Jackson

The Erie Canal

The Erie Canal stretched from Buffalo to Albany, New York. This was a major undertaking in our nation's transportation industry. This canal would cover over 350 miles and allowed cargo to be shipped across the entire length of New York. It also brought new cities to New York and increased the state's population.

This canal project was known as Clinton's Big Ditch. The canal was crucial to America's transportation system because it demonstrated that America had the ingenuity to construct such projects. Goods could be shipped faster and cheaper by boat than by wagon.

Instructions: Sequence the events of building the Erie Canal.

Chapter 5: Expansion and Reform (1835-1869)

The policy known as Manifest Destiny truly defines the political philosophy of President Polk. Americans had the view that this entire land was theirs to settle from the Atlantic to the Pacific. The discovery of gold in California did more to settle the West than any other single event. It was during this period that social reformers emerged; they began to address some of society's problems and inequities.

★ Verbal/Linguistic ★

1 Explain the concept of Manifest Destiny.

2 Discuss the impact that the Seneca Falls Conference had upon the Suffrage Movement.

3 Discuss how the Manifest Destiny affected the institution of slavery.

4 Complete a descriptive writing activity about social reformers of this period.

5 Write a story about travel on the Oregon Trail.

6 Write a letter about the discovery of gold in California.

7 Create a crossword puzzle about James K. Polk.

8 Complete a creative writing exercise about pioneer women.

9 Write a play about a family's decision to head westward in pursuit of gold.

10 Write a newspaper article about the Mexican War.

11 Write a speech that details how Manifest Destiny affected Native Americans.

★ Logical/Mathematical ★

1 List facts about the Oregon Trail.

2 Classify and categorize materials taken on the Oregon Trail.

3 Graph America's population shift from 1835 to 1869.

4 Sequence the major events of Manifest Destiny on a time line.

5 Discover and report on any political or economic patterns in Manifest Destiny.

6 Predict why the Transcontinental Railroad began in the North.

7 Compare and contrast the impact that Manifest Destiny had upon Native Americans and slaves.

8 Determine and discuss how the Kansas-Nebraska Act changed the Missouri Compromise.

9 Evaluate the value of the Gadsden Purchase.

10 Describe in detail how Manifest Destiny affected the abolitionists.

11 Graph the depletion of buffalo in the Great Plains from 1840-1869. Describe the effect on Native Americans who lived there.

Experience U.S. History! • Rickey Millwood
Kagan Publishing • 1 (800) 933-2667 • www.KaganOnline.com

Visual/Spatial

1 Design a postcard about Manifest Destiny.

2 Watch a video on the Oregon Trail.

3 Design a postage stamp about the 1848 Seneca Falls Conference.

4 Draw a scene, illustrating how Native Americans were affected by Manifest Destiny.

5 Create an advertisement for supplies needed for the Oregon Trail.

6 Create a flier advertising St. Joseph, Missouri, as a starting place for the Oregon Trail.

7 Create a painting or drawing of a wagon train passing through American Indian Territory.

8 Design a newspaper headline about the outbreak of the Mexican War.

9 Make a poster about the role women played in Manifest Destiny.

10 Create an illustration of the disputed Oregon Territory.

Musical/Rhythmic

1 Listen to songs performed along the Oregon Trail.

2 Listen to railroad songs.

3 Research music sung in Southern churches just before the Civil War erupted.

4 Perform a song sung by slaves on Southern plantations.

5 Interpret the meaning of the songs about the Underground Railroad.

6 Write a song about one major event from 1835 to 1869.

7 Identify any changes in musical instruments during the 1840s.

8 Identify any songs that enticed people to head for California in search for gold.

9 Imagine you were a song writer during the period of Manifest Destiny. What would be the major theme in your music?

10 Identify musical instruments played by Native Americans who lived on the plains.

Chapter 5 continued
Expansion and Reform
(1835-1869)

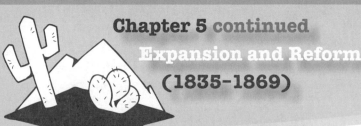

⭐ Bodily/Kinesthetic

1 Role-play Neal Dow in his stand for Prohibition.

2 Act out the role of Elizabeth Cady Stanton at the Seneca Falls Conference.

3 Act out the role of Frederick Douglas at the Seneca Falls Conference.

4 Act out the role of a pioneer woman on the Oregon Trail.

5 Act out the roles of Native Americans and pioneers as covered wagons pass through American Indian Territory.

6 Perform a skit about the Grimke sisters and their abolitionist views.

7 Perform a dance done on the Oregon Trail.

8 Act out the role of Sam Houston after Texas was granted independence.

9 Perform a skit about the discovery of gold in California.

10 Create models of tools used by Western miners.

11 Construct a pan that could be used by miners to sift for gold.

12 Role-play James K. Polk in a campaign speech.

⭐ Naturalist

1 Observe a ring around the full moon in the winter, indicating approaching snow.

2 Record changes in the terrain as a result of the Oregon Trail.

3 Record changes in the slave population due to expansion into Texas.

4 Observe buffalo in a natural park or on the Internet.

5 List characteristics of the Plains Territory.

6 Record changes in America's size as a result of Manifest Destiny.

7 Examine a cotton ball and feel the seeds.

8 Visit the Alamo in San Antonio, Texas. Or visit the official website.

9 Visit the Arch of St. Louis—Gateway to the West.

10 Sort and categorize the tools used by Western miners.

11 Examine pictures from the Internet of the Western mountains crossed by pioneers.

12 View cactus in the Southwest in the vicinity of the Gadsden Purchase.

13 Record the function of each part of a covered wagon.

14 Observe and report on how the Mississippi River was used to transport cotton to the gulf.

15 Record the changes in the soil due to the continual planting of cotton.

Experience U.S. History! • **Rickey Millwood**
Kagan Publishing • 1 (800) 933-2667 • www.KaganOnline.com

Interpersonal

1 Interview each other about the views of Neal Dow.

2 Debate how Manifest Destiny was positive and negative for the nation.

3 Solve the conflict between Native Americans and pioneers driving wagon trains through American Indian Territory.

4 Debate the decision by Texans to defend the Alamo at all costs.

5 Take turns giving examples of Manifest Destiny.

6 Share with others your opinion about building the Transcontinental Railroad.

7 Condemn or praise the Declaration of Sentiments passed at the Seneca Falls Conference.

8 Discuss with a partner the major implications from the Seneca Falls Conference.

9 Share with others your thoughts on the California Gold Rush.

10 Reach a consensus on why America needed a Transcontinental Railroad.

Intrapersonal

1 Observe and discuss attitude changes in women as a result of the Seneca Falls Conference.

2 Describe your feelings about the expansion of slavery into Texas.

3 Choose between defending the Alamo or surrendering it to General Santa Anna.

4 Express your likes and dislikes about the ideas of Neal Dow.

5 Weigh alternatives to taking wagon trains through hostile American Indian Territory.

6 Think about the actions of Zachary Taylor in the Mexican War.

7 Defend the position to admit California as a free, rather than slave, state.

8 Describe your feelings about settlers from the East rushing to the West in an attempt to strike it rich.

9 Form an action plan to prevent the expansion of slavery into the West.

10 Write about the actions of James Polk as president.

Experience U.S. History! • Rickey Millwood
Kagan Publishing • 1 (800) 933-2667 • www.KaganOnline.com

5.1 Blackline Master • Verbal/Linguistic Activity

Expansion and Reform

The Fall of the Alamo

Completely surrounded and realizing that no help was coming, the brave Alamo defenders must have been frightened. They had bought 13 precious days for Sam Houston and Texas. The 180 plus defenders were badly outnumbered and fought against overwhelming odds. On March 6, 1836, the Alamo finally fell to the Mexican General Santa Anna.

Santa Anna meant to crush the rebellion in Texas and retain Texas as a part of Mexico. All defenders of the Alamo were put to death. Santa Anna raised a red flag, which signaled no mercy, and had his band play the horrifying song "Deguello". Santa Anna allowed a few slaves and woman to leave the Alamo to warn others of his bloody tactics.

The defenders hurt Santa Anna by inflicting serious damage to his army. Soon Sam Houston captured Santa Anna after defeating his army at San Jacinto.

Instructions: Imagine that Santa Anna was placed on trial for war crimes at the Alamo. Suppose he butchered those few soldiers that surrendered, including Davy Crockett. On a separate sheet of paper, write the transcript from a trial held to determine if Santa Anna was guilty. Which actor should play each role? Write your choice by each character.

- Santa Anna _____
- Alamo survivors _____
- Mexican soldiers _____
- Prosecution team _____
- Defense team _____
- Jury _____
- Judge _____
- Sam Houston _____

Expansion and Reform

The Oregon Trail

The Oregon Trail was an overland route to the West, beginning in Missouri. This expedition usually took six months and covered 2,000 miles. Wagon trains, often pulled by oxen, moved slowly and had to begin in the spring.

It was crucial that pioneers cross the mountains in California before the snow came each fall. The trip was extremely dangerous as the wagons passed through hostile territory. The pioneers also had to contend with other hardships such as sickness. These elements claimed many people. Bodies were buried all along the trail. Yet, brave pioneers took the trail to go West.

Activity Options

1. Do a team PowerPoint presentation about the Oregon Trail and its importance in American history.

2. Role-play a wagon master negotiating a deal with Native Americans to allow the wagons to pass through their territory.

3. Using a musical instrument, play a song that was played along the Oregon Trail.

4. Role-play pioneers discussing the possibility of making a trip to California on the Oregon Trail.

5.3 Blackline Master • Interpersonal Activity

Expansion and Reform

The Gadsden Purchase

After the Mexican War, and as a result of gold being discovered in California, a southern route to California was sought. Mexico owned a strip of land greatly desired by the United States. In the Gadsden purchase, a class example of Manifest Destiny, the United States bought a strip of land from Mexico for $10 million. This purchase would allow a railroad to be constructed from Texas to California. Settlers and materials could move quickly through the Southwest to California.

Instructions: Debate the Gadsden Purchase. Use this page to organize your thoughts before the debate.

_____
_____
_____
_____
_____
_____
_____
_____
_____
_____
_____
_____

Expansion and Reform

The Gold Rush

Imagine hearing stories of finding gold in California. The prospect to strike it rich was a big temptation for many. So, a massive migration to the West took place.

The discovery of gold did more to settle California than any other factor. California quickly became a state. Other strikes in the West brought an onrush of prospectors to Colorado and Nevada as well. Mining towns sprang up and prospered until the mines went dry. Some towns thrived while others became ghost towns. The miner led the way for future settlements in the West. Life would change forever for the Native Americans who already lived in the West.

Instructions: Compare and contrast mining in the 1850s and in the present.

1850	Present
Mining Equipment	
Effect on the Environment	
Mining Safety	
Mineral Extraction	
Government Regulations	

Chapter 6
The Peculiar Institution and the Causes of the Civil War
(1840-1865)

Several major causes led to the Civil War, including the institution of slavery. This social evil had existed since the Colonial period and now had expanded into Texas. The invention of the cotton gin fostered slavery in the deep South. It would take the shedding of blood to bring the issue to a final conclusion.

Verbal/Linguistic

1 Discuss how cotton became "King" across the entire South after 1800.

2 Read *Uncle Tom's Cabin*.

3 Share ideas about the Fugitive Slave Act.

4 Debate the motives in John Brown's raid on Harper's Ferry.

5 Write an essay about Frederick Douglas.

6 Write a research paper about the Dred Scott case.

7 Discuss Susan B. Anthony as an abolitionist.

8 Complete a creative writing essay about Harriet Tubman.

9 Read John Blasingame's book *The Slave Community*.

10 Read and write an essay about Nat Turner's Rebellion.

11 Discuss the implications of the Kansas-Nebraska Act.

12 Discuss the decision by South Carolina to leave the Union after Lincoln was elected.

13 Discuss the advantages of the North going into the Civil War.

14 Describe the Anaconda Plan of Abraham Lincoln.

Logical/Mathematical

1 Predict the implications and repercussions of the Kansas-Nebraska Act.

2 Sequence the political mistakes that led to the Civil War between 1840-1860.

3 Graph the economic differences between the North and South in 1860.

4 Calculate the number of slaves that escaped from the South between 1840 and 1865.

5 Discover patterns toward abolition in the Border States.

6 Organize facts about the Fugitive Slave Act.

7 Brainstorm ideas about the conductors that operated the Underground Railroad.

8 Examine the results of the 1860 presidential election.

9 Assess the decision by South Carolina to secede from the Union after President Lincoln was elected.

10 Compile facts about the transportation system in the South in 1860.

11 Analyze the disadvantages of the South entering the war.

12 Estimate the number of bales of cotton per year the entire South was producing on the eve of the war.

Visual/Spatial

1 Draw a political cartoon about Popular Sovereignty.

2 Make a PowerPoint of the major causes of the Civil War.

3 Design a flier urging volunteers to join the Union Army.

4 Design a map that illustrates the trails of the Underground Railroad.

5 Create a newspaper article as written by William Lloyd Garrison.

6 Design a postcard about the antebellum South.

7 Create a crossword puzzle about the politicians from the Civil War era.

8 Watch a video on the Underground Railroad.

9 Draw a scene of something that led to the Civil War.

10 Draw a political cartoon about "Bleeding Kansas".

11 Create a PowerPoint about John Brown's raid on Harpers Ferry.

12 Create a PowerPoint about South Carolina's secession from the Union.

13 Watch the film *Uncle Tom's Cabin*.

14 Watch the film *Gone with the Wind*.

Musical/Rhythmic

1 Determine why slaves were not allowed to have loud instruments on plantations.

2 Find a picture of musical instruments used on plantations in the antebellum South.

3 Identify any songs about the coming of the Civil War.

4 Interpret the lyrics to the song "Follow the Drinking Gourd."

5 Interpret the lyrics of and then sing the song, "John Brown's Body."

6 Play a song on a banjo from the antebellum period.

7 Interpret the spirituals sung on Southern plantations by slaves prior to the Civil War.

8 Evaluate church music in the antebellum South.

9 Compose a melody about a major event that caused the Civil War.

10 Write a song about the election of Abraham Lincoln.

11 Learn about the minstrel shows during the antebellum period.

12 Perform any popular dance prior to the Civil War.

Chapter 6 continued

The Peculiar Institution and the Causes of the Civil War (1840-1865)

Bodily/Kinesthetic

1 Act out the role of Frederick Douglas as an abolitionist.

2 Act out the role of Harriet Tubman as a conductor on the Underground Railroad.

3 Perform a skit about the Underground Railroad.

4 Build a model of an antebellum Southern plantation.

5 Act out the role of a Southern secessionist after Lincoln was elected.

6 Act out the role of Judge Roger Taney in the Dred Scott case.

7 Role-play William Lloyd Garrison as editor of the *Liberator*.

8 Role-play Senator Charles Sumner hurling insults at the South that brought on the attack by Preston Brooks.

9 Role-play John Brown at his trial.

10 Role-play Susan B. Anthony as an abolitionist.

Naturalist

1 Visit Fort Sumter in historic Charleston, South Carolina.

2 Trace the routes of the Underground Railroad.

3 List the characteristics of the antebellum South.

4 Observe fields of cotton growing. Write about your experience.

5 Examine pictures of a cotton gin.

6 Visit a plantation manor in the South.

7 Observe the rivers and mountains that led into the South.

8 Observe the Big Dipper, which was used by slaves escaping on the Underground Railroad.

9 Visit the historic rail center at Chattanooga, Tennessee.

10 Build a model of a log cabin.

11 Record changes in the Industrial North from 1840 to 1860.

12 Prepare a typical meal eaten by an American in 1860.

Experience U.S. History! • Rickey Millwood
Kagan Publishing • 1 (800) 933-2667 • www.KaganOnline.com

1 Debate the immediate effects of Nat Turner's Rebellion.

2 Interview each other about the major causes of the Civil War.

3 Share with others your feelings about the antebellum South.

4 Do a team presentation on the new weapons that were used in the Civil War.

5 Write a collaborative paper on South Carolina's decision to secede from the Union.

6 Discuss with a partner the advantages of the North going into the war.

7 Address, in groups of four, the major problems the South faced going into the Civil War.

8 Reach a consensus on the importance of the Dred Scott Decision.

9 Do a team presentation on medical practices prior to the Civil War.

10 Role-play General Lee as he decides which side to take.

11 Criticize the decisions that led to the Civil War.

12 Share with others why the Civil War would last nearly five years.

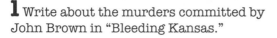

1 Write about the murders committed by John Brown in "Bleeding Kansas."

2 Make an action plan of escape on the Underground Railroad.

3 Defend the position by Harriet Tubman to help runaway slaves.

4 Observe and discuss mood changes in the North after the Fugitive Slave Act was passed.

5 Describe your feelings about the abolitionist John Brown.

6 Compare and contrast the Missouri Compromise with the Kansas-Nebraska Act.

7 Write about the actions of Preston Brooks as he caned senator Charles Sumner.

8 Express your likes and dislikes about President James Buchanan.

9 Describe your feelings about the nation entering the Civil War in 1861.

10 Weigh alternatives to the Civil War.

11 Write about the actions of the Southern states after Lincoln was elected.

12 Discuss the actions of Southerners toward William Lloyd Garrison.

13 Write about the impact of *Uncle Tom's Cabin*.

14 Interpret the mood changes in the nation from 1850 to 1860.

Experience U.S. History! • **Rickey Millwood**
Kagan Publishing • 1 (800) 933-2667 • www.KaganOnline.com

6.1 Blackline Master • Musical/Rhythmic Activity

The Peculiar Institution and the Causes of the Civil War

The Underground Railroad

By the eve of the Civil War, there were more than three million slaves in the South. Thousands of slaves fled the South to escape this miserable form of human bondage. The Underground Railroad was a system of routes that led slaves.

Stations or hiding places were set up along various routes for runaway slaves.

Those that helped slaves escape conductors were often runaways themselves. Harriet Tubman was one of these brave individuals. She put herself at risk many times to help others escape. The song, "Follow The Drinking Gourd" is about the Underground Railroad. Its lyrics have hidden meanings that helped slaves escape to freedom.

Instructions: Write a song about the Underground Railroad.

6.2 Blackline Master • Verbal/Linguistic Activity

The Peculiar Institution and the Causes of the Civil War

The Abolitionist Movement

The Abolitionist Movement was led by people such as William Lloyd Garrison, Frederick Douglas, Susan B. Anthony, Harriet Tubman, Sojourner Truth, and John Brown. The most recognized abolitionist newspapers were the *North Star* and the *Liberator*. Literature such as *Uncle Tom's Cabin* by Harriet Beecher Stowe, caused Southerners to be especially angry with Northerners.

The Compromise of 1850 only furthered the abolitionists' anger as part of the compromise contained the Fugitive Slave Act. New slave hunters could go into the North to retrieve slaves.

Instructions: Build a word web around the concept of abolition.

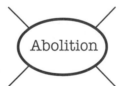

6.3 Blackline Master • Bodily/Kinesthetic Activities

The Peculiar Institution and the Causes of the Civil War

The Dred Scott Case

One of the most important decisions by the Supreme Court concerning slavery was the Dred Scott case. According to Dred Scott, a slave, he should be allowed to go free because his owner took him above the Missouri Compromise line of 36° 30'N. In fact, he had lived in a free state for more than a year.

Judge Roger Taney was the Supreme Court chief justice in this famous case. The court ruled against Dred Scott and stated that Scott was property of the owner. The court also ruled the Missouri Compromise to be illegal. The court decided that Congress could not make laws that told individuals where they could or could not take their property. Southerners were delighted with the ruling; abolitionists were furious. The nation was moving closer to war.

Activity Options

1. Debate the Dred Scott Decision.

2. Re-enact the Dred Scott trial.

3. Role-play abolitionists after hearing the Dred Scott ruling.

Experience U.S. History! • Rickey Millwood
Kagan Publishing • 1 (800) 933-2667 • www.KaganOnline.com

6.4 Blackline Master • Visual/Spatial Activity

The Peculiar Institution and the Causes of the Civil War

The Caning of Senator Charles Sumner

In Congress, tempers reached the point of open aggression as Senator Charles Sumner of Massachusetts, an abolitionist, offended Senator Butler of South Carolina. Senator Sumner made disparaging remarks toward the South. Senator Butler had a cousin, Preston Brooks, who served in the House of Representatives. Brooks was determined to defend his aging cousin who was very popular in the U.S. Senate. So, Brooks went to the Senate and attacked Senator Sumner with a cane. He stated that he whipped him with a cane as he thought of Sumner as a dog due to his insults.

Northerners were offended by the attack, and Southerners were glad that Brooks taught Sumner a lesson. This was a prelude for the Civil War. The next series of fights between Americans would soon begin at a place called Fort Sumter.

Instructions: Create a political cartoon of the confrontation between Charles Sumner and Preston Brooks.

Chapter 7

The Civil War and Reconstruction

(1861–1877)

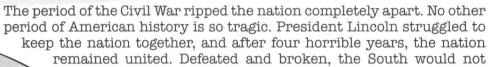

The period of the Civil War ripped the nation completely apart. No other period of American history is so tragic. President Lincoln struggled to keep the nation together, and after four horrible years, the nation remained united. Defeated and broken, the South would not recover for decades. The conclusion of the war brought three new amendments that affected slaves. African Americans were now free citizens of the United States. The process of healing through Reconstruction would be slow, and the South would not see all federal troops removed until 1877.

Verbal/Linguistic

1 Read *The Killer Angels*.

2 Share ideas about the strategy of the Confederate States in conducting the war.

3 Complete a descriptive writing exercise about the Presidential election of 1876.

4 Compare and contrast the *Monitor* and *Merrimac*.

5 Discuss the effects of Lincoln's Emancipation Proclamation.

6 Debate the strategy of Robert E. Lee to invade Maryland.

7 Compare and contrast women in the North and South during the Civil War.

8 Write a research paper on a Civil War battle.

9 Discuss the diplomacy of King Cotton.

10 Explain the concept of Reconstruction.

11 Read about the Freeman's Bureau.

12 Write a newspaper article about President Andrew Johnson's impeachment and trial.

Logical/Mathematical

1 Sequence the major battles of the Civil War.

2 Evaluate the ideas of the radical Republicans during Reconstruction.

3 Categorize the weapons used in the Civil War.

4 Calculate the deaths in the Civil War prison camps of Andersonville, Fort Delaware, and El Mira.

5 Compare and contrast Generals Lee and Grant.

6 List and organize facts about Sherman's March through Georgia.

7 Sequence the major Reconstruction Acts after 1865.

8 Describe how the end of the Civil War affected African Americans.

9 Make predictions about the economic conditions in the South after the war ended.

10 Use inductive reasoning to determine why women were not given the right to vote in the 15th Amendment.

11 Discover patterns in Congress during Reconstruction.

Experience U.S. History! • Rickey Millwood
Kagan Publishing • 1 (800) 933-2667 • www.KaganOnline.com

★ Visual/Spatial ★

1 Watch the film *Gettysburg*.

2 Watch the film *Glory*.

3 Imagine, and then write about, your life as a soldier in the Civil War.

4 Create a PowerPoint about medical practices during the Civil War.

5 Draw a scene from a Civil War battle.

6 Make a poster that illustrates a time line of the Civil War.

7 Examine photographs on the Internet of soldiers that fought in the Civil War.

8 Draw a scene about Lincoln's Emancipation Proclamation.

9 Create a PowerPoint about the generals of the Civil War.

10 Watch the film *Andersonville*.

11 Draw a scene from Sherman's March through Georgia.

12 Make a poster of the Reconstruction presidents.

13 Watch the film *Gone with the Wind*.

14 Watch the film *The Red Badge of Courage*.

★ Musical/Rhythmic ★

1 Listen to the "Battle Hymn of the Republic."

2 Research the origin of the song "Dixie."

3 Research the role of drummers in Civil War battles.

4 Listen to the song, "The Night They Drove Old Dixie Down" by Joan Baez.

5 Listen to the "Bonnie Blue Flag."

6 Listen to "When Johnny Comes Marching Home".

7 Listen to "Marching Through Georgia."

8 Learn about the musical instruments played by soldiers in the Civil War.

9 Research the pitch and rhythm of the "Rebel Yell" by Confederate soldiers.

10 Write a song about the role of women in the Civil War.

11 Write a song about Lee's surrender at Appomattox.

12 On an instrument, for the class play a song from the Civil War.

Experience U.S. History! • Rickey Millwood
Kagan Publishing • 1 (800) 933-2667 • www.KaganOnline.com

Chapter 7 continued
The Civil War and Reconstruction (1861–1877)

Bodily/Kinesthetic

1 Visit Fort Sumter in Charleston, South Carolina.

2 Act out the role of a secessionist as the Civil War erupts.

3 Perform a skit about a Southern family just hearing the news about Gettysburg.

4 Act out the role of a survivor of Andersonville Prison.

5 Role-play Abraham Lincoln giving the Gettysburg Address.

6 Role-play a family in Georgia just before the arrival of General Sherman.

7 Role-play General Lee surrendering to General Grant.

8 Visit any Civil War battlefield or museum.

9 Role-play Confederate and Union soldiers at a 50-year reunion.

10 Practice the "Rebel Yell."

Naturalist

1 Capture the landscape and terrain of a Civil War battlefield in photographs.

2 Observe pictures of Civil War monuments. Describe them to a partner.

3 Take a walking tour through a Civil War battlefield.

4 Classify the materials used to color Confederate uniforms.

5 Record changes in the diet of soldiers, based upon the season.

6 Record changes in cotton production in the South immediately following the war.

7 Classify the materials used to build the ironclad ships.

8 Observe Vicksburg on the Mississippi River.

9 Travel through the Shenandoah Valley.

10 Visit the grave site of any Civil War general.

11 Observe natural materials used to build fortifications in Civil War battles.

12 Visit the Confederate Museum in Richmond, Virginia.

Experience U.S. History! • Rickey Millwood
Kagan Publishing • 1 (800) 933-2667 • www.KaganOnline.com

Interpersonal

1 Discuss with a partner the strategy of the South entering the war.

2 Do a team presentation on a Civil War battle and its impact.

3 Do a team presentation of Sherman's March through Georgia.

4 Discuss as a class the conditions in Civil War prisons.

5 Take turns, criticizing General Burnside's decisions at Fredericksburg.

6 Share with a partner about Lincoln's determination to find a fighting general.

7 Reach a consensus on the Confederate failure on the third day at Gettysburg.

8 Write a report on a Civil War field hospital.

9 Write a report on the weapons used in the Civil War.

10 Role-play any Civil War person and have class members interview him or her.

11 Address the major problems the South faced after the Civil War.

12 Do a team presentation on several major Reconstruction Acts.

13 Discuss the impeachment of President Andrew Johnson.

14 Interview each other about the outcome of the 1876 presidential election.

Intrapersonal

1 Describe your feelings about the Civil War.

2 Express your likes and dislikes about Robert E. Lee.

3 Write an ethical code of conduct for the prisoners in Civil War prisons.

4 Take a stance for the 13th and 14th Amendments.

5 Write about the actions of John Wilkes Booth in his assassination of President Lincoln.

6 Defend the position by President Johnson not to follow the Tenure Act.

7 Weigh alternatives to the impeachment of President Johnson.

8 Prioritize the needs of the nation at the conclusion of the Civil War.

9 Write about the needs of recently freed slaves at the conclusion of the war.

10 Describe your feelings about the Grant presidency.

11 Think about and discuss the actions of Congress in deciding the 1876 election.

12 Mediate on the Compromise of '77.

13 Defend the position to keep federal troops in the South until 1877.

14 Make an action plan that would prevent secession from happening again.

Experience U.S. History! • Rickey Millwood
Kagan Publishing • 1 (800) 933-2667 • www.KaganOnline.com

7.1 Blackline Master • Verbal/Linguistic Activity

The Civil War and Reconstruction

Bull Run

The first shots of the Civil War were fired at Fort Sumter, but the first major land engagement took place in Virginia. Many people came to see the first battle at Bull Run in April 1861. It was believed by many that the Southern army would be routed and that this would be a short war.

The nation was stunned because the Confederates won this first major engagement. This battle brought General Thomas "Stonewall" Jackson into prominence. He would be General Lee's right arm until he was shot by mistake.

Bull Run was just the beginning of this nightmare in American history. Bloody battles in places such as Shiloh and Antietam would soon follow.

EXTRA!!   EXTRA!!

Instructions: Write a newspaper article about the outcome of Bull Run.

The Civil War and Reconstruction

The North and the South

The North had great advantages over the South as the Civil War began. Almost all of the nation's industry was located in the North. The North also produced much of the nation's food. Many slaves that escaped also fought against the Confederacy. On the other hand, the South had excellent generals and a strong will. That great amount of determination eventually crumbled. General Robert E. Lee invaded the North twice but was beaten back at Antietam and Gettysburg.

Most rebellions are not successful without foreign intervention. The South took a gamble that France and Britain would enter on their behalf since they depended on "King Cotton". That was not to be the case. Britain and France had plenty of cotton stored and had foreign supplies.

Instructions: Create a chart to show the cost of the Civil War in dollars and lives.

The Civil War and Reconstruction

Sherman's March

Cutting a trail of devastation and sheer terror, General William T. Sherman rode through the South. After burning Atlanta, Sherman determined to bring the Confederacy to its knees and headed through Georgia to the coast. The Union Army burned, plundered, and emancipated slaves all through the South. Plantation owners pleaded for their homes, livestock, and food, but this was total war. It may have been General Sherman who said, "war is hell." Slaves ran to General Sherman as they were now at last free from the bondage of human misery. Lincoln's Emancipation now had the meaning he desired years earlier.

Why did General Sherman wage such a brutal war against civilians? Sherman felt that if he could wage such a war, the will to fight on in the South would cease. In December 1864, Sherman arrived in Savannah and telegraphed Lincoln that the capture of Savannah was Lincoln's Christmas present. Then, the Union Army headed for South Carolina. The South was worn down and could no longer continue to fight. By April 1865, the war ended with Grant accepting Lee's surrender at Appomattox, Virginia.

Instructions: Write an ethical code of conduct that General Sherman could have implemented toward Southern civilians.

Code of Conduct

The Civil War and Reconstruction

The Freeman's Bureau

Slaves that had been recently emancipated soon faced immense obstacles. Many were hungry, homeless, and had only agricultural skills. Freedom came with a price as the South was in total devastation. How would the federal government assist these recently freed people other than through written amendments?

The federal government decided to establish the Freeman's Bureau to assist the recently freed slaves just months before the war ended. This agency helped to feed, clothe, and educate helpless individuals. The Bureau achieved its greatest success in the field of education, with thousands being schooled.

Many Southerners deeply resented this agency, and it ceased in 1872. But it did serve a major function in providing services to those in desperate need.

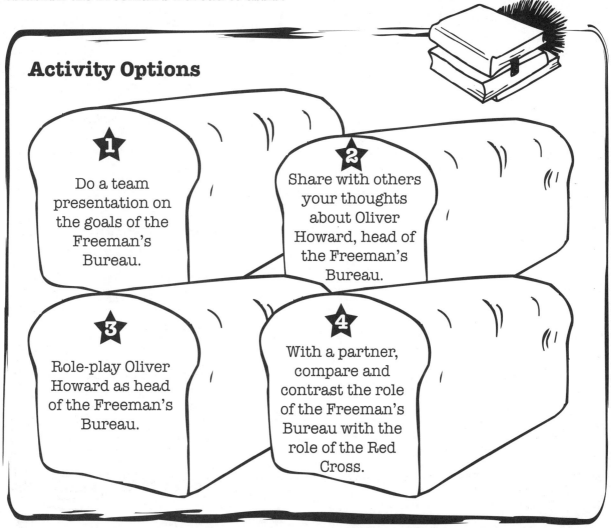

Activity Options

1. Do a team presentation on the goals of the Freeman's Bureau.

2. Share with others your thoughts about Oliver Howard, head of the Freeman's Bureau.

3. Role-play Oliver Howard as head of the Freeman's Bureau.

4. With a partner, compare and contrast the role of the Freeman's Bureau with the role of the Red Cross.

Chapter 8
The American West
(1865-1900)

Settlers rushed westward in order to strike it rich. Some did, but most were unfortunate. This massive migration to the West had many consequences. The Indian Wars erupted and the western Native Americans were forced off their lands and onto reservations. Other settlers moved west and began herding cattle, which was made possible by the new invention of barbwire. This period is marked by the Transcontinental Railroad—a system of transportation that linked the entire nation.

Verbal/Linguistic

1 Write a narrative about the construction of the Transcontinental Railroad.

2 Write General George Custer's or Chief Sitting Bull's obituary.

3 Write a story about traveling on a wagon train to California.

4 Complete a descriptive writing exercise about the Battle of the Little Big Horn.

5 Tell a story about the Ghost Dance Movement.

6 Discuss Frederick Jackson Turner's Frontier Thesis.

7 Write a poem about a great Native American chief.

8 Write a diary entry of one Pony Express rider's day.

9 Debate the government's decision to place Native Americans on reservations.

10 Read Helen Hunt Jackson's *A Century of Dishonor*.

11 Write an essay describing the impact of the Gold Rush on the nation.

Logical/Mathematical

1 List and organize facts about Western cowboys.

2 Calculate the time and money needed to complete the Transcontinental Railroad.

3 Classify and categorize materials and supplies needed to build the Transcontinental Railroad.

4 Make predictions about how barbwire would tame the West.

5 Compare and contrast weapons used by the U.S. cavalry and Native Americans.

6 Graph how the buffalo was depleted from 1865 until 1900.

7 Sequence the major events in the West from 1849 until 1900.

8 Make associations between ghost towns and mining towns.

9 Calculate the ratio of participants on each side of the Battle of the Little Big Horn.

10 Estimate the amount of gold and silver extracted from the West from 1849 until 1900.

11 Assess the impact that strip mining had upon the environment of the Western states.

12 List and organize facts about cattle drives from Texas to Kansas.

Experience U.S. History! • Rickey Millwood
Kagan Publishing • 1 (800) 933-2667 • www.KaganOnline.com

⭐ Visual/Spatial ⭐

1 Design a poster that advertises for Pony Express riders.

2 Create a political cartoon of a gold prospector that struck it rich.

3 Design a brochure, advertising for railroad workers.

4 Draw a scene of a ghost town.

5 Examine pictures that demonstrate Western attire.

6 Draw a picture of settlers traveling in a wagon train westward through American Indian Territory.

7 Design a postcard showing scenes of wildlife in the West.

8 Create a scene about barbwire in the West.

9 Design a postage stamp, depicting a major event in the history of the West.

10 Create a map and label the major Western Native American tribes on the map.

⭐ Musical/Rhythmic ⭐

1 Classify five songs according to various topics about the West.

2 Discuss the importance that music had upon the West.

3 Listen to three Western ballads.

4 Listen to three songs about cattle drives.

5 Compose a jingle about products a miner would purchase.

6 Listen to three songs about railroad construction.

7 Compose a song about the Transcontinental Railroad.

8 Compose a song about Custer's Last Stand.

9 Describe several types of instruments played on the Oregon Trail.

10 Theorize how music romanticizes the West.

11 Study the importance of the Ghost Dance Movement.

12 Report on the type of music and dance the Western Native Americans performed in their ceremonies.

13 Listen to one song about a Western hero.

14 Have the school band, orchestra, or chorus perform a concert of Western songs.

Experience U.S. History! • Rickey Millwood
Kagan Publishing • 1 (800) 933-2667 • www.KaganOnline.com

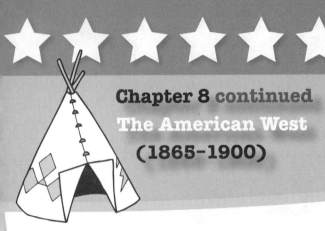

Chapter 8 continued
The American West
(1865–1900)

Bodily/Kinesthetic

1 Perform a skit about the completion of the Transcontinental Railroad.

2 Role-play the ghost of General Custer. Have students interview the ghost to learn about the Battle of Little Big Horn.

3 Act out the role of a prospector that just found gold.

4 Act out the role of Native American chief after seeing the buffalo being eradicated.

5 Role-play Chief Joseph or Sitting Bull and have other students interview him.

6 Act out the role of a telegraph operator and practice learning Morse code.

7 Build a model of a Native American dwelling.

8 Perform a type of dance that settlers performed around campfires on the Oregon Trail.

9 Build a model of a Conestoga wagon.

10 Build a model of a pan used by prospectors to search for gold.

11 Visit the National Museum of the American Indian in Washington DC.

Naturalist

1 Describe the major physical features of the West.

2 Classify mountain ranges settlers crossed on their way to California.

3 Classify the types of vegetation in the Western states.

4 Describe any natural phenomena such as geysers.

5 Visit a historical sight in the West.

6 Observe a circle around a full moon in the winter, indicating an approaching snowstorm.

7 Categorize materials carried in covered wagons along the Oregon Trail.

8 Map out the trail used by Pony Express riders.

9 Visit museums in Western states and examine artifacts of Native Americans.

10 Determine and discuss how barbwire changed ranching practices in the West.

Experience U.S. History! • **Rickey Millwood**
Kagan Publishing • 1 (800) 933-2667 • www.KaganOnline.com

Interpersonal

1 Discuss with a partner the importance of the Transcontinental Railroad.

2 Share with others the hardships that pioneers faced on the trails to California.

3 Do a team presentation on the Donner family.

4 Write a collaborative report on the importance of the buffalo to the Native Americans.

5 Interview each other about California's quick admission into the Union.

6 Discuss with a partner the difficulties of a cattle drive from Texas to Kansas.

7 Reach a consensus on why cowboys participated on dangerous cattle drives.

8 Make a team project on one Native American tribe.

9 Criticize the government's breaking of treaties with Native Americans.

10 Take turns sharing interesting information about events in the West.

Intrapersonal

1 Write an ethical code of conduct that should have been implemented toward the Native Americans in the West.

2 In an essay, defend the position to build the Transcontinental Railroad.

3 Respond to the dilemma to build the Transcontinental Railroad through American Indian Territory.

4 Prioritize the items settlers would have taken on a wagon train across the West.

5 Write about the actions of Chief Joseph.

6 Write about the needs of Native Americans after first being placed on reservations.

7 Write about the military actions of Crazy Horse and Sitting Bull.

8 Think about the role William Cody played in the West. Then write a short note thanking him for this contribution.

9 Observe and discuss the mood changes in the East once gold was discovered in California.

10 Write about the responsibilities of a wagon train master.

11 Make a journal entry as if you were a woman heading West on a wagon train.

12 Write about actions the Native Americans took to preserve their way of life in the West.

Experience U.S. History! • Rickey Millwood
Kagan Publishing • 1 (800) 933-2667 • www.KaganOnline.com

8.1 Blackline Master • Bodily/Kinesthetic Activity

The American West

The Western Miners

The discovery of gold and silver in the West did more to settle the region than any other factor. The population of California, Nevada, and Colorado exploded due to the discovery of these minerals. Mining towns sprang up everywhere and prospered until the vanes went dry. Towns were then abandoned and became ghost towns.

People in the East heard of these strikes and headed West to make their fortunes. Farmers and ranchers soon followed, but it was the miner and prospector that led the way to settle the West.

Instructions: Perform a skit about a family planning to move to California after the discovery of gold.

The American West

The Pony Express

The ancient Inca had a system of relay runners that could deliver messages hundreds of miles away. In the United States, a similar system would be tried—the Pony Express. It was short-lived and put out of business by the telegram; the Express only existed from April 1860 until October 1861.

The Pony Express delivered mail from St. Joseph, Missouri, to Sacramento, California. A series of about 80 relay riders covered a distance of 1,900 miles in 10 days. These were extremely dangerous rides due to bandits and Native Americans. A typical rider could earn about $100 a month and cover nearly 80 miles a day. Relay stations were set up along the route so that riders and horses could be changed quickly. A rider would stop for a fresh horse after about then miles.

Instructions: Design a map that shows the route of the Pony Express.

The American West

The Transcontinental Railroad

America was finally united from coast to coast when the Transcontinental Railroad was completed in 1869 at Promontory Point, Utah. This great railroad had been constructed by the Union and Central Pacific Railroad companies. The railroad healed the wounds of the nation that had been caused by the Civil War by uniting the country. Civil War veterans worked side by side on America's greatest construction project.

The railroad was positive in that it linked the nation. Americans could travel from coast to coast, and goods could be shipped along the route. However, it was also detrimental. Native Americans suffered greatly because the railroad went through their territory. In addition, buffalo hunters eradicated the buffalo to feed railroad workers and deprive Native Americans of food. The railroad brought thousands of setters into the West and the Indian Wars soon followed. Wagon trains would pass through, but they were not permanent. The railroad was there to stay. Native Americans referred to it as the Iron horse.

Chinese workers were used for the Central Pacific line. They made excellent workers for the railroad company. They used picks and shovels and hacked trails through dangerous mountains in California. They were responsible for the railroad passing through regions where most people thought it could not be constructed. Shortly after the completion of the railroad, the Chinese Exclusion Act was passed. They were the first group in America to have immigration restrictions against them. Miners did not want the Chinese prospecting in areas where they lived.

Instructions: On a separate sheet of paper, write an essay that expresses your likes and dislikes about the construction of the Transcontinental Railroad. Consider all the consequences and implications from building this railroad. Record some ideas below.

_____
_____
_____
_____
_____
_____
_____

8.4 Blackline Master • Interpersonal Activity

The American West

The Cattle Drives

The cattle drive had a tremendous impact on the West. Texas contained several million head of wild longhorn cattle. Cattle were rounded up, as they would bring a good market price, then moved northward. Once the cattle were rounded up, cattle drives would begin toward the holding corrals in Kansas. From Kansas, cattle were shipped by rail to the great slaughter and meat-packing houses of Chicago. These were dangerous trips. Many cowboys were former slaves.

Joseph Glidden's invention of barbwire soon made it possible for the ranching business to exist. Barbwire meant that large areas of land could be fenced in and cattle could be contained and managed. This wire did more to tame the Wild West than any other invention. A severe blizzard in the 1880s caused herds of wild cattle to die off. But barbwire meant that ranchers no longer had to depend on cattle drives. New strains of cattle were bred and soon the cattle drives completely stopped.

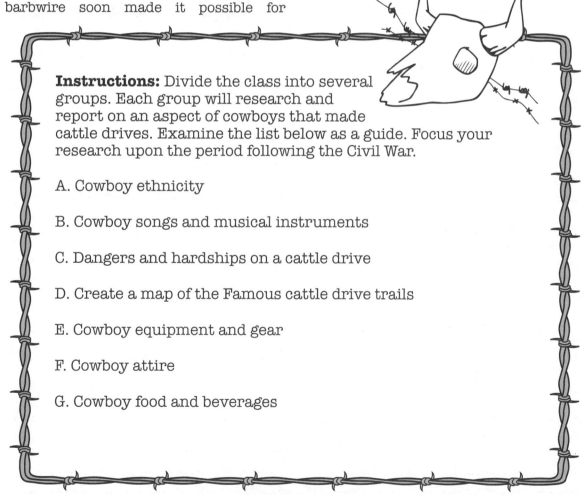

Instructions: Divide the class into several groups. Each group will research and report on an aspect of cowboys that made cattle drives. Examine the list below as a guide. Focus your research upon the period following the Civil War.

A. Cowboy ethnicity

B. Cowboy songs and musical instruments

C. Dangers and hardships on a cattle drive

D. Create a map of the Famous cattle drive trails

E. Cowboy equipment and gear

F. Cowboy attire

G. Cowboy food and beverages

Experience U.S. History! • Rickey Millwood

Chapter 9

The Gilded Age
(1877–1900)

The Gilded Age demonstrates a period of rapid growth in America, which brought both prosperity and problems. America really began to exert its industrial strength and potential during this period. This era is marked by the Robber Barons, labor strikes, and currency issues. Recently freed slaves still had obstacles that confronted them in the form of the Jim Crow laws.

Verbal/Linguistic

1 Analyze the phrase *Gilded Age*.

2 Share ideas about the characteristics of the Robber Barons.

3 Compare and contrast any two Robber Barons.

4 Write a speech about a major invention during the Gilded Age.

5 Debate the outcome of the 1876 presidential election.

6 Discuss how the Gilded Age changed life in American cities.

7 Write a paper about the needs of average Americans during the Gilded Age.

8 Write a persuasive paper urging President Hayes to remove the last federal troops from the South.

9 Explain the concept of Social Darwinism.

10 Discuss how Carnegie's steel industry impacted railroad construction.

11 Write a newspaper article about the Haymarket Riot in Chicago.

12 Compare and contrast the Grange Movement with the Populist Party.

Logical/Mathematical

1 Graph patterns of population movement during the Gilded Age.

2 Analyze data about the expansion of railroads from 1865 to 1900.

3 Discover patterns in how the Robber Barons made their fortunes.

4 Calculate the probability that the Knights of Labor were involved in the Haymarket Riot.

5 Determine the speed that a telegraph could travel across the nation.

6 Sequence the major political events of the Gilded Age.

7 Analyze financial information about the Panic of 1893.

8 Create a chart that demonstrates immigration to America from 1877 to 1900.

9 Make predictions about the problems that rapid industrialization would bring to America.

10 Brainstorm ideas about the Cross of Gold Speech.

Experience U.S. History! • Rickey Millwood
Kagan Publishing • 1 (800) 933-2667 • www.KaganOnline.com

Visual/Spatial

1 Draw a political cartoon about a Robber Baron.

2 Design a scene about Grange meetings.

3 Draw a scene of an industrial factory, spotlighting a worker.

4 Make a poster in support of the Knights of Labor.

5 Sketch of a new invention in the Gilded Age.

6 Draw a political cartoon for the phrase "Rum, Romanism, and Rebellion".

7 Create a PowerPoint about the Gilded Age.

8 Pretend to be a philanthropist from the Gilded Age.

9 Create a political cartoon of the Gold Bugs.

10 Design a brochure about any resort during the Gilded Age.

11 Draw a scene of the Pullman Strike.

12 Create a picture of society benefiting from the Captains of Industry.

13 Create a political cartoon of the Sherman Antitrust Act.

14 Create an illustration in support of the Pendleton Act.

Musical/Rhythmic

1 Write a song that satirizes the Gilded Age.

2 Determine patterns in music from 1870 to 1900.

3 Identify any new musical instruments during the Gilded Age.

4 Determine how music changed for freed slaves after the Civil War.

5 Interpret the meaning to the words of the song, "Eight Hours."

6 Play an instrument for your class that was invented during the Gilded Age.

7 Compare and contrast music of the industrial cities to music of the rural areas.

8 Determine the type of music one president of the Gilded Age enjoyed.

Chapter 9 continued
The Gilded Age
(1877–1900)

Bodily/Kinesthetic

1 Act out the role of a Robber Baron as a philanthropist.

2 Perform a skit about Coxey's March of the unemployed on Washington DC.

3 Act out the concept of Social Darwinism.

4 Role-play J. D. Rockefeller attempting to buy out a competitor.

5 Act out the role of an industrial factory worker trying to support a large family.

6 Act out the role of a child exploited by the coal industry.

7 Role-play Eugene Debs and his involvement in the Pullman Strike.

8 Role-play the candidates in the 1896 election.

9 Act out the role during a campaign of a Populist political candidate.

10 Perform a skit about the rise of Populism.

Naturalist

1 List the changes in the American terrain as a result of drilling for oil.

2 Classify the traits of an urban area as a result of rapid industrialization.

3 Categorize the minerals necessary for the production of steel.

4 Record changes in mining procedures as a result of the growth of steel mills in Pennsylvania.

5 Categorize the animals affected by railroad construction.

6 Find pictures of harbors and rivers that are dredged for shipping. Write about possible environmental consequences of this action.

7 Record the changes in the depletion of minerals during the Gilded Age.

8 Record how the color of brick changed in industrial towns as a result of the burning of coal.

9 Classify the health problems caused by the breathing of iron impurities in a steel mill.

10 Discuss the changes in agricultural practices due to the invention of new equipment in the Gilded Age.

Experience U.S. History! • **Rickey Millwood**
Kagan Publishing • 1 (800) 933-2667 • www.KaganOnline.com

Interpersonal

1 Discuss with a partner the major changes in America during the Gilded Age.

2 Interview each other about how cities changed as a result of rapid industrialization.

3 Share with others the major problems caused by industrialization.

4 Reach a consensus explaining why the government sided with industry when labor strikes erupted.

5 Role-play, then mediate, the conflict of the Pullman Strike.

6 Write a collaborative paper about the issues of the 1896 election.

7 Do a team presentation on one major type of industry during the Gilded Age.

8 Solve a simulated conflict over the pollution of a city's water supply as a result of industrialization.

9 Do a team presentation on the role of women during the Gilded Age.

10 Discuss with a partner why large numbers of African Americans moved to the North during the Gilded Age.

Intrapersonal

1 Describe your feelings about one of the Robber Barons.

2 Express your likes and dislikes about the way the government handles labor strikes.

3 Describe your feelings about the Knights of Labor and the Haymarket Riot.

4 Take a stand to support the action of President Cleveland in the Pullman Strike.

5 Observe and discuss the changes in the lives of women during the Gilded Age.

6 Write an ethical code of rules the Robber Barons could follow in regard to protecting the environment.

7 Write about the consequences that resulted when James Blaine used the phrase, "Rum, Romanism, and Rebellion."

8 Write about your wants and needs as an African American in the Gilded Age.

9 Choose between keeping the Spoils System in politics or enacting the Pendleton Act.

10 Write about the actions of Henry Clay Frick during the Carnegie Steel Mill Strike.

Experience U.S. History! • Rickey Millwood

The Gilded Age

Who Were the Robber Barons?

Great fortunes were made by a few men during the Gilded Age. America began to show some signs of wealth during this period, but much of the county remained mired in poverty. Just a few individuals controlled most of the nation's oil, steel, railroads, and money. These include John D. Rockefeller, J. P. Morgan, Andrew Carnegie, and Cornelius Vanderbilt. How did these men outperform their competition? How were they able to build these great fortunes?

The concept to survive and outperform your rivals in business and industry is called Social Darwinism. These businessmen believed that they were more flexible and smarter than their competition. When necessary, these individuals could be ruthless and crush competitors.

A belief existed that God had made these businessmen wealthy, and they should return some of this money to society. They gave hundreds of millions away to colleges and charities. So, how do we judge these men? Were they Robber Barons or Captains of Industry?

Instructions: List and organize facts about four Robber Barons.

John D. Rockefeller

J. P. Morgan

Andrew Carnegie

Cornelius Vanderbilt

Experience U.S. History! • **Rickey Millwood**
Kagan Publishing • 1 (800) 933-2667 • www.KaganOnline.com

9.2 Blackline Master • Interpersonal Activity

The Gilded Age

The Great Labor Strikes

Violence erupted across America several times during the Gilded Age. It was a confrontation between labor and business in a changing America. Industrialization brought many changes so quickly that a spectrum of problems developed. Four major strikes took place, and each time the government sided with industry instead of organized labor. How could the government side with ruthless business practices?

America was following the business philosophy of laissez faire economics. This belief stated that the government should keep its hands off the economy and let the businessmen manage the nation's wealth. But during the Gilded Age, labor began to organize on an immense scale. Labor unions, such as the Grange, Knights of Labor, and American Federation of Labor, were formed. A clash between industry and labor was inevitable.

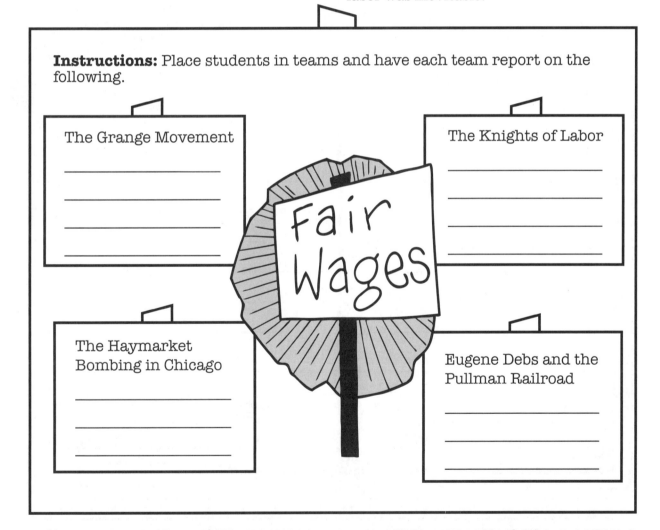

Instructions: Place students in teams and have each team report on the following.

- The Grange Movement
- The Knights of Labor
- The Haymarket Bombing in Chicago
- Eugene Debs and the Pullman Railroad

Experience U.S. History! • Rickey Millwood
Kagan Publishing • 1 (800) 933-2667 • www.KaganOnline.com

9.3 Blackline Master • Verbal/Linguistic Activity

The Gilded Age

The Jim Crow Laws

African Americans continued to suffer in the Gilded Age as a result of measures called the Jim Crow laws. These were laws that suppressed people who had been slaves or children of slaves and restricted voting in a number of ways. African Americans could not vote if they could not read in Southern states. Even if they could pass a literacy test, they still faced poll taxes and threats in the form of beatings. The federal troops had been removed from the South by President Hayes and no federal authority was around to help minorities. The matter was made even worse with the court case *Plessy v. Ferguson* in 1896. The Supreme Court ruled that separate but equal was legal between the races. This case was more of a setback to African Americans than any other case in the nation's history. This case would not be reversed until *Brown v. Board of Education* in 1954.

Instructions: Write, then discuss, the implications of *Plessy v. Ferguson*.

9.4 Blackline Master • Visual/Spatial Activity

The Gilded Age

The Gilded Age Puzzle

The Gilded Age demonstrates a period of rapid growth in American history. The nation was changing from a rural economy to an industrial giant. America forged ahead of the rest of the world.

Americans experienced political, economic, and social change as the nation emerged in full gear toward the beginning of a new century. Enormous fortunes were made by businessmen like Carnegie and Vanderbilt. In the meantime, politicians argued over gold and silver issues.

Instructions: Create a crossword puzzle using each of the following Gilded Age terms.

John D. Rockefeller	Samuel Gompers
Haymarket Riot	Jim Crow
Andrew Carnegie	Cross of Gold
Social Darwinism	Mugwumps
Pendleton Act	Chester Arthur
Spoils System	James Blaine
James Garfield	Mark Twain
Gold Bugs	Grover Cleveland
Pullman Strike	Mary Eddy
Knights of Labor	Jane Addams

Experience U.S. History! • Rickey Millwood
Kagan Publishing • 1 (800) 933-2667 • www.KaganOnline.com

Chapter 10: The Progressive Movement and Foreign Affairs (1900-1918)

Progressive reformers vigorously attacked the social, political, and economic evils that were deeply rooted in American culture. They made tremendous strides in many areas, including labor and industry. Reporters and photographers took assertive roles in exposing the ills of society through their writings and pictures. This movement achieved success through the administrations of Roosevelt, Taft, and Wilson.

★ Verbal/Linguistic ★

1 Share ideas about muckrakers and their mission to rid society of evils.

2 Read and discuss *The Jungle* by Upton Sinclair.

3 Write a report on Ida Tarbell.

4 Discuss the major goals of the Progressives.

5 Explain why the Progressive Movement began in the Northeast.

6 Write a persuasive paper advocating the end of child labor in 1910.

7 Compare and contrast the Progressive policies of Presidents Roosevelt, Wilson, and Taft.

8 Create a slogan about the idealism of the Progressives.

9 Write a newspaper article about a major accomplishment of the Progressives.

10 Write a play about the writers of *McClure's Magazine*.

11 Communicate ideas about yellow journalism.

12 Write a summary of the affect the Spanish American War had upon the nation.

★ Logical/Mathematical ★

1 Sequence the major accomplishments of the Progressives on a time line from 1900 until America's entry into World War I.

2 Classify the various types of Progressives.

3 Organize facts about the goals and reforms of the Progressives.

4 Discover any patterns in the policies of U.S. presidents toward trust busting.

5 Brainstorm ideas about "Fighting" Robert Lafollette of Wisconsin.

6 Determine how the exposé of Ida Tarbell affected the business of Standard Oil Company.

7 Predict how the coming of World War I affected child labor.

8 Evaluate the major reasons why the Progressives challenged major companies.

9 Analyze data about the social issues the Progressives confronted.

10 Synthesize ideas about reforms made in the meat-packing industry as a result of the novel *The Jungle*.

Experience U.S. History! • Rickey Millwood
Kagan Publishing • 1 (800) 933-2667 • www.KaganOnline.com

Visual/Spatial

1 Research and analyze five political cartoons about child labor.

2 Examine photographs taken by Lewis Hine, of children employed in dangerous capacities.

3 Draw a political cartoon of Teddy Roosevelt as a trust buster.

4 Draw a scene of a Muckraker investing in a particular industry.

5 Draw a political cartoon advocating for the 17th Amendment.

6 Create a graphic organizer promoting passage of the 18th Amendment.

7 Draw a political cartoon of Susan B. Anthony discussing suffrage with President Teddy Roosevelt.

8 Make a poster advocating the passage of the 19th Amendment.

9 Create a PowerPoint about the Triangle Shirtwaist Fire.

Musical/Rhythmic

1 Listen to ragtime music.

2 Listen to the song "Maple Leaf Rag" by, Scott Joplin.

3 Play for the class a song by Scott Joplin.

4 Evaluate the dominant instruments in ragtime music.

5 Research and perform the fox trot dance for the class.

6 Listen to the music of Irving Berlin.

7 Interpret the lyrics to "Alexander's Ragtime Band" by Irving Berlin.

8 Evaluate ragtime music and determine its influence on jazz music.

9 Learn about the instruments used to play ragtime music.

10 Take a popular song today and perform it in the style of the Progressive Age.

Chapter 10 continued
The Progressive Movement and Foreign Affairs (1900–1918)

★ Bodily/Kinesthetic

1 Role-play Ida Tarbell as she investigates Standard Oil.

2 Perform a skit about the meat-packing industry before passage of the Pure Food and Drug Act.

3 Role-play a child employed in a Southern textile mill around 1910.

4 Role-play Lewis Hine as he gains entry into a steel mill employing children.

5 Act out the role of a newspaper investigator examining the abuses of public utilities.

6 Role-play Bob Lafollette advocating for the regulation of railroad rates.

7 Act out the role of women in Wyoming voting for the first time.

8 Create a skit of Populists and Progressives meeting and discussing their reform goals.

9 Act out the concept of "muckraking."

10 Role-play Alice Paul and Carrie Catt in their role to promote the Suffrage Movement.

★ Naturalist

1 List the characteristics of a large industrialized city before the Progressive Movement around 1900.

2 Record the changes the Progressive made in cleaning up the industrial cities.

3 Discuss the policies of Gifford Pinochet, the director of the U.S. Forest Service.

4 Evaluate President Taft's decision to open Alaskan wilderness to public developers.

5 Record how the terrain of Panama was affected by the building of a canal during the presidency of Teddy Roosevelt.

6 Determine how Dr. William Gorgas eliminated malaria and yellow fever from Panama.

7 View a video illustrating the construction of the Panama Canal.

8 Find a picture that illustrates how the locks operate the flow of water at the Panama Canal. Describe the process in writing.

9 Determine how the president wanted to use America's resources but also wanted to protect the environment and natural beauty.

10 Locate pictures of children working with bales of cotton stacked in a Southern textile mills. Write a diary entry as if you were one of these children, describing your work.

11 Locate pictures of children working in fish-packing houses and oyster beds in Alabama and Mississippi.

12 Discuss the impact that the Newlands Act of 1902 had upon the deserts of the Southwest.

Experience U.S. History! • **Rickey Millwood**
Kagan Publishing • 1 (800) 933-2667 • www.KaganOnline.com

 Interpersonal

1 Share with others the main goals of the Progressive Movement.

2 Discuss with a partner why the Progressive Movement was primarily an upper middle class movement.

3 Take turns naming the major problems America faced from 1900–1917.

4 Interview each other about why America was slow to end child labor.

5 Write a collaborative paper on the photographs of Lewis Hine.

6 Mediate a solution to the anthracite coal strike.

7 Criticize the industrial giants who brought many social problems to industrial cities.

8 Criticize the nation for allowing child labor to exist until the 1920s.

9 Reach a consensus on the major accomplishments of the Progressives.

10 Do a team presentation on the most important pieces of legislation passed between the years of 1900–1917.

11 Role-play a writer at *McClure's Magazine*. Motivate others in a crusade against social evils.

12 Reach a consensus explaining why the 18th, 19th, and 20th Amendments were passed.

 Intrapersonal

1 Describe your feelings about the creation of America's national parks during the Progressive Age.

2 Think about the actions of President Roosevelt in trust busting. Share your thoughts with a partner.

3 Make an action plan for cleaning up the meat-packing industry in 1906.

4 Prioritize the agenda for the elimination of America's social problems from 1900–1917.

5 After creating a plus/minus chart choose between the alternatives of eliminating child labor or industrial output.

6 Write an ethical code for children working in 1900.

7 Write about the actions of the progressives after Gifford Pinchot was dismissed.

8 Write an editorial about Civil Rights during the Progressive Age after the landmark Supreme Court decision of *Plessy v. Ferguson*.

9 Write about the actions of President Wilson as a Progressive.

10 Express your likes and dislikes about Prohibition and the 18th Amendment.

11 Take a stance to support the policies of the Progressives.

12 Observe the mood of legislators to prevent another disaster like the Triangle Shirt Sweatshop Fire of 1911.

10.1 Blackline Master • Visual/Spatial Activity

The Progressive Movement and Foreign Affairs

Child Labor

Child labor was the social evil the Progressives had the least success in trying to eliminate. Too many people across America were desperate for money and saw nothing wrong with children working. Little children were denied their education and the right to their childhood. Covered with blood from injuries, the children labored through long, difficult days. The rapid development of heavy industry in the North and cotton mills in the South put these children in extremely dangerous jobs.

The Social reformer and photographer, Lewis Hine used his camera to expose this evil. He photographed thousands of the child laborers. But his gallant effort fell short of ending this evil. Basically, the thought was that since children had mouths, they could work for their food. Unfortunately, World War I prolonged child labor.

Instructions: Design a poster exposing the evils of child labor. Draft your ideas below.

Experience U.S. History! • Rickey Millwood
Kagan Publishing • 1 (800) 933-2667 • www.KaganOnline.com

10.2 Blackline Master • Interpersonal Activities

The Progressive Movement and Foreign Affairs

The Muckrakers

The *muckrakers* were a group of reporters that fought against social evils. Through their writing they desperately tried to improve society. These muckrakers, such as Upton Sinclair and Ida Tarbell, drew awareness issues that shocked Americans. *McClure's Magazine* was well known for its muckraking articles. President Teddy Roosevelt was greatly disturbed by Sinclair's *The Jungle*. This book led to new laws for food safety. The nation owes much to these writers and to politicians such as Wisconsin's "Fighting" Bob Lafollette.

Activity Options

1. Do a team presentation on the most serious problems in America in 1900 that were addressed by the Progressives.

2. Imagine the year is 1910. Role-play several muckrakers and report your findings to the class.

3. Reach a consensus on which social problems need addressing in America today. Then, divide the class into teams and have each group write an exposé on a different problem.

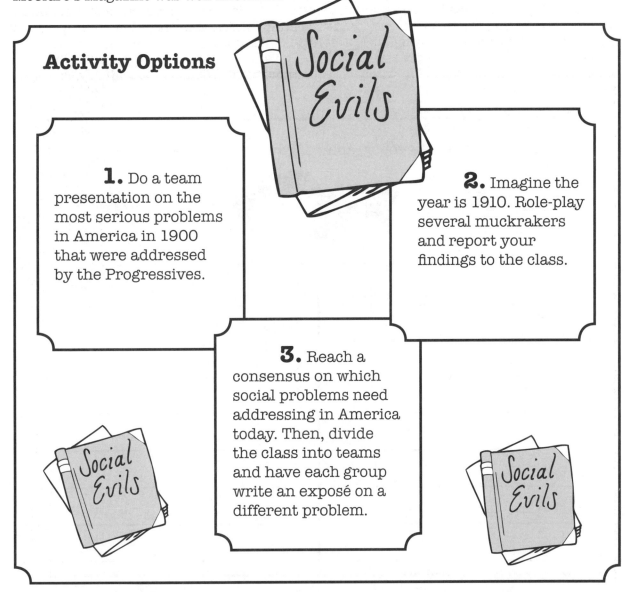

Experience U.S. History! • Rickey Millwood
Kagan Publishing • 1 (800) 933-2667 • www.KaganOnline.com

10.3 Blackline Master • Naturalist Activity

The Progressive Movement and Foreign Affairs

The Panama Canal

The construction of the Panama Canal illustrates a determination and ingenuity never seen before in American history. A canal slicing through malaria-infested jungles would save thousands of miles of sea travel around South America. President Teddy Roosevelt was convinced that a canal through the Isthmus of Panama would be vital to America's security, so he seized the Canal Zone. He later admitted, "I took the isthmus."

It was an enormous task digging through 40 miles of mud and rock. Workers suffered from insect bites and the blistering heat of Panama. Dr. Gorgas made the canal safer for workers by implementing a number of measures to prevent malaria. Engineers constructed giant locks, which lift and lower ships that enter and exit the canal. Today, the Panama Canal remains one of the most impressive architectural feats in the world.

Instructions: Describe the topography of Panama. List the characteristics of the weather in Panama.

Topography	Weather
_____	_____
_____	_____
_____	_____
_____	_____
_____	_____
_____	_____
_____	_____
_____	_____

Experience U.S. History! • Rickey Millwood
Kagan Publishing • 1 (800) 933-2667 • www.KaganOnline.com

10.4 Blackline Master • Bodily/Kinesthetic Activities

The Progressive Movement and Foreign Affairs

Prohibition

Prohibition crusaders believed that alcoholism contributed to abuse and unemployment; they thought America would be a more moral nation without alcohol and set out to eliminate this demon. Women were fully behind Prohibition because their husbands were the only source of income. Many women felt that if alcohol were eliminated from society, their husbands would work regularly and abuse toward them would cease.

The Temperance Movement, social crusaders, and churches finally achieved their goal after decades of hard work. This came with the 18th Amendment, which prohibited the sale or consumption of alcoholic beverages. This amendment would be enforced by the Volstead Act.

Eliminating alcohol from society was not practical. Prohibition—a noble experiment turned into a fiasco. Trying to completely close down all establishments that sold alcoholic beverages was impossible. No amount of law enforcement could keep people from drinking. In fact, Prohibition paved the way for gangsters to control alcohol. Smuggling whiskey in from the West Indies was rampant. In 1933, after years of failure, the government repealed the 18th Amendment with the 21st Amendment.

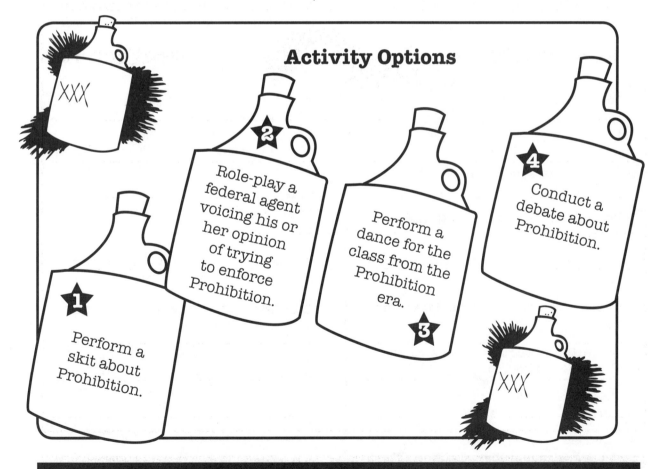

Activity Options

1. Perform a skit about Prohibition.
2. Role-play a federal agent voicing his or her opinion of trying to enforce Prohibition.
3. Perform a dance for the class from the Prohibition era.
4. Conduct a debate about Prohibition.

Chapter 11: The Era of World War I (1914-1919)

America remained neutral when World War I erupted. Events, such as the Zimmermann Telegram and the German policy of unrestricted submarine warfare, finally pulled America into the conflict. America won the Great War and emerged from the conflict as the world's strongest nation. A League of Nations was formed after the war to keep world peace, but the United States never joined. The United States would again return to a policy of isolationism.

Verbal/Linguistic

1 Debate the decision by President Wilson for the United States to remain neutral at the beginning of World War I.

2 Discuss the impact that the sinking of the *Lusitania* had upon the American people.

3 Share ideas about the new weapons used in World War I.

4 Write a poem about the horror of No Man's Land.

5 Write a newspaper article about the Zimmermann Note.

6 Explain the concept of unrestricted submarine warfare.

7 Write a letter protesting the Sedition and Espionage Acts.

8 Read and analyze the stipulations of the Versailles Treaty.

9 Debate the decision by Congress not to join the League of Nations.

10 Read the novel *All Is Quiet on the Western Front*.

11 Discuss the impact of the Spanish influenza epidemic at the end of World War I.

Logical/Mathematical

1 Sequence the major events that led America into World War I.

2 Symbolize in numbers the ethnic groups from America that fought in World War I.

3 Calculate the probability of being drafted into the U.S. Army in 1917.

4 Graph the causalities that the United States sustained in World War I.

5 Compare and contrast the sinking of the *Lusitania* with the sinking of the *Titanic*.

6 Make predictions about how the lives of Americans changed as the nation entered World War I.

7 Analyze the data about African American units that fought in World War I.

8 Classify and categorize the equipment American soldiers were issued.

9 List and organize facts about the preparation of the American military as the nation entered World War I.

10 Evaluate the ideas by President Wilson to make a "peace without victory."

11 Solve the problem to transport the U.S. Army to the European theater of war.

Experience U.S. History! • Rickey Millwood
Kagan Publishing • 1 (800) 933-2667 • www.KaganOnline.com

Visual/Spatial

1 View the film *Sergeant York*.

2 Create a political cartoon about the sinking of the *Lusitania*.

3 View the film *Paths of Glory*.

4 Examine photographs of No Man's Land.

5 Design a postage stamp about World War I.

6 Draw a scene about America's entry into World War I.

7 Create a PowerPoint of the new weapons and technology used in World War I.

8 Watch the film *All Is Quiet on the Western Front*.

9 Create a scene of how the airplane was used in World War I.

10 Draw a scene illustrating sacrifices made by American consumers in World War I.

11 Examine pictures of uniforms worn in World War I. Compare the uniforms to those worn in the Revolutionary War.

12 Make a poster urging for or against America's entry into the League of Nations.

Musical/Rhythmic

1 Listen and interpret the song lyrics to "Over There."

2 Sing the song "Goodbye Broadway, Hello France."

3 Listen and interpret the lyrics to the song, "Mademoiselle from Armentiers."

4 Listen to and interpret the song, "It's a Long Way to Tipperary."

5 Determine the influence Big Band music had upon World War I.

6 Compose a song about the sinking of the *Lusitania*.

7 Evaluate music about World War I.

8 Write a song about America's entry into World War I.

9 Listen to American, French, and German songs played during World War I.

10 Perform as a class several songs played during World War I.

Chapter 11 continued
The Era of World War I
(1914–1919)

★ Bodily/Kinesthetic

1 Act out the role of President Wilson after hearing the news of the sinking of the *Lusitania*.

2 Act out President Wilson asking for a declaration of war against Germany.

3 Perform a skit about the Zimmermann Note.

4 Visit a monument that honors soldiers that fought in World War I.

5 Act out the role of an American soldier in the trenches of World War I.

6 Role-play a survivor from the *Lusitania* and describe what happened to the ship.

7 Build a model of No Man's Land.

8 Perform a dance from the era of World War I.

9 Create a poster urging Americans to be patriotic during World War I.

10 Role-play the Big Four at the Paris Peace Conference.

11 Role-play Congress debating and voting on America's entry into the League of Nations.

12 Role-play soldiers from the different nations that fought in World War I and tell their experiences before the class.

13 Visit a World War I battlefield in Europe.

14 Role-play a soldier that was a victim of a gas attack in the trenches of France.

15 Create a project about the medical advances during World War I.

★ Naturalist

1 List the characteristics of No Man's Land.

2 Research the conditions of the ocean when the *Lusitania* sank.

3 Record the changes in the terrain of Europe by 1918.

4 Examine pictures of the trenches of World War I. Explain how the trenches were used.

5 Categorize the materials found in No Man's Land.

6 Find pictures of the trenches of World War I filled with water. Research the problems this water caused.

7 Find a picture of soldiers covered with snow in World War I. Determine the impact weather had on soldiers in World War I.

8 Find a picture of merchant marine survivors in a life raft floating on the icy Atlantic. Discuss with a partner how the survivors might have felt.

9 View photos of trench rodents.

10 Devise a classification system that illustrates the price of vegetables during World War I.

88 **Experience U.S. History!** • **Rickey Millwood**
Kagan Publishing • 1 (800) 933-2667 • www.KaganOnline.com

1 Debate the issue of America's neutrality at the beginning of World War I.

2 Do a team presentation on prices and wages during World War I.

3 Interview a partner in the role of Teddy Roosevelt after the sinking of the *Lusitania*.

4 Write a term paper on how World War I changed America.

5 Share with others your likes and dislikes about President Wilson.

6 Do a team presentation on the propaganda slogans used in World War I.

7 Prioritize the major goals of preparing the nation for World War I.

8 Mediate the conflict in the Supreme Court case *Schenck v. the United States*.

9 Interview each other about the conservation of certain foods during the war.

10 Promote the purchase of Liberty Bonds as a Hollywood movie star.

11 Do a team presentation on African American units that fought in World War I.

12 Share with each other information about the Espionage and Sedition Acts.

13 Interview each other about the way World War I was resolved.

14 Do a team presentation about the new weapons used in World War I.

15 Share your thoughts about the Versailles Treaty and how Germany was punished at the conclusion of World War I.

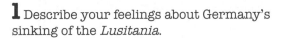

1 Describe your feelings about Germany's sinking of the *Lusitania*.

2 Describe your feelings about President Wilson's decision to keep America out of the conflict until 1917.

3 Observe and describe the mood changes in Americans after the declaration of war.

4 Mediate on how World War I affected African Americans.

5 Think about the actions of women that worked in factories during World War I. Write about their contributions to the war effort.

6 Write an ethical code of conduct toward the treatment of prisoners of war.

7 Express your likes and dislikes about President Wilson.

8 Express your likes and dislikes about the Espionage and Sedition Acts.

9 Choose between entering the conflict in 1917 or completely staying out of the war. Explain your reasoning.

10 Defend the position of General Pershing to use African Americans in combat missions.

11 Write about the actions of the Creel Committee.

12 Relate the sinking of the *Lusitania* to the attack on America on 9-11.

13 Observe and discuss the mood changes in Americans at the conclusion of the war.

14 Make an action plan to prevent another World War.

Experience U.S. History! • Rickey Millwood
Kagan Publishing • 1 (800) 933-2667 • www.KaganOnline.com

The Era of the World War I

The Sinking of the *Lusitania*

Lurking near the coast of Ireland in 1915 were German submarines or u-boats. These u-boats were trying to cut supply lines between the United States and Britain. They inflicted tremendous damage on ships that were believed to be carrying cargo to Britain. In May 1915, Germany warned that any ships in the war zone would be torpedoed. Kaiser Wilhelm of Germany was well aware of this warning.

The warning from Germany was ignored and the cruise ship *Lusitania*, departed from New York. The ship crossed the Atlantic and was just a few miles from Ireland when a German submarine sank it. Over 1,000 passengers died, including more than 100 Americans. Americans were furious that the Germans had attacked a civilian ship. The Germans believed the *Lusitania* was carrying large amounts of ammunition.

Unrestricted submarine warfare by Germany was effective but highly risky. Would the United States now enter the war? The American public was livid, but President Wilson did not want to go to war over this isolated incident. However, Germany continued this practice and in 1917, the United States entered the fray.

Instructions: Create a political cartoon about Kaiser Wilhelm and the *Lusitania*.

11.2 Blackline Master • Intrapersonal Activity

The Era of the World War I

Trench Warfare

Soldiers standing in icy water with artillery shells landing among them were ghastly scenes from World War I. These were the conditions endured by the brave men that served all nations. This great adventure, as it was called in 1914, turned into an absolute nightmare. World War I introduced the world to new and untested weapons. These weapons had enormous killing power and resulted in millions of deaths.

President Wilson kept the nation out of the war as long as possible. America refrained from this conflict until 1917, when it entered the Great War. Unrestricted submarine warfare and the Zimmermann note were both instrumental in pulling the United States into the conflict.

After winning bloody battles in France, the United States emerged the victor. The German will to fight was broken by the sheer number of Americans. On November 11, 1918, an armistice was signed and the war ended. The United States emerged as the world's strongest nation, but this war was settled in such a way that it gave rise to a Second World War only 20 years later.

Instructions: Imagine you were a soldier in the trenches of World War I. Respond to the dilemma of being sent across No Man's Land.

11.3 Blackline Master • Musical/Rhythmic Activity

The Era of the World War I

Songs of Patriotism

Our emotions and feelings can be deeply touched when our nation enters war. Songs provide an expression of the event, and there are plenty of patriotic songs from the World War I era. All Americans were expected to be in support of the war and the music of the time certainly reflects that position.

World War I demonstrates how patriotic songs can inspire soldiers and civilians in times of crisis. Americans heard songs that stirred their emotions such as the popular, "Over There" by George M. Cohan. This was the most popular song of the entire war. Mr. Cohan was recognized many years later by Congress for his patriotism in writing this song.

Instructions: Write a song about World War I.

The Era of World War I

Ending the War

America's entry into the Great War turned the tide in favor of the Allies. The Central Powers collapsed after being overwhelmed by Americans. In 1918, it was all over, but the difficult decision of peace-making followed.

President Wilson went to the Paris Peace Conference with his Fourteen Points. He urged for a "peace without victory." He felt that it would not be wise to make a harsh and bitter treaty toward Germany. Both the French and British wanted to ensure Germany paid a heavy price. Germany had the Versailles Treaty forced upon her, and the seeds of revenge and hatred were planted. Germany felt humiliation and anger by having no say in the treaty stipulations.

What would the future hold for a defeated Germany? How long would Germany wait before starting another war? The rise of Adolf Hitler and the Third Reich would soon address the Versailles issue. It's hard to believe that another world conflict would come only 20 years after World War I. Would a fair and just treaty have prevented this? Historians still ponder that very question today.

Activity Options

1. Role-play the various nations that made up the Versailles treaty and discuss their positions.

2. In pairs, take turns criticizing the harsh stipulations in the Treaty of Versailles.

3. Reach a consensus as a class on a treaty that would have been reasonable for Germany to accept after World War I.

4. As a small group, brainstorm ideas that would have prevented World War II.

5. Role-play diplomats and form a solution to the conflict in Iraq.

Chapter 12: The Roaring '20s (1920-1929)

The Roaring '20s capture our imagination as a time of excitement and a flowering of the arts. Artists poured into Harlem and produced some of the finest works of literature in American history. Americans were enjoying themselves and witnessed events such as Lindbergh's flight and Babe Ruth's baseball career. By the end of the decade, the prosperity would vanish and the nation would enter a dismal time we call the Great Depression.

Verbal/Linguistic

1 Analyze the phrase "The Roaring '20s.

2 Discuss how the 19th Amendment affected the 1920 election.

3 Write a newspaper article about the Prohibition.

4 Read a book about gangsters of the 1920s.

5 Write a report about the evolution of jazz music.

6 Do a creative writing exercise about Henry Ford and his Model T automobile.

7 Write a research paper on the changing image of women in the 1920s.

8 Make a word web about sports heroes from the 1920s.

9 Tell a story about Amelia Earhart.

10 Write a letter describing Charles Lindbergh's crossing of the Atlantic aboard the "Spirit of St. Louis."

Logical/Mathematical

1 Sequence the major inventions that changed America during the 1920s.

2 Graph the stock market rise from 1920 to 1928 and the subsequent crash.

3 List and organize facts about Prohibition.

4 Brainstorm ideas about the changes in automobiles during the 1920s.

5 Analyze data about the 1924 election.

6 Create a chart that demonstrates the growth of the National Association for the Advancement of Colored People by 1920.

7 Discuss trends in crimes related to Prohibition.

8 Create a biographical timeline about Margaret Sanger.

9 Synthesize ideas about the changing morals of the 1920s.

10 Identify the causes of the Stock Market Crash.

11 Compare and contrast the personalities of Marcus Garvey, Booker T. Washington, and W. E. B. Dubois.

12 Calculate the distance Charles Lindbergh flew across the Atlantic Ocean.

Experience U.S. History! • Rickey Millwood
Kagan Publishing • 1 (800) 933-2667 • www.KaganOnline.com

Visual/Spatial

1 Draw a political cartoon of Al Capone.

2 Design a postcard about a major event from the 1920s.

3 Design a brochure about the "flapper."

4 Design a poster about members of the 1927 New York Yankee baseball team.

5 Design a skyscraper that would give a large city a distinct appearance.

6 Draw a scene of women voting in the 1920 election.

7 Draw a picture of clothing worn in the 1920s.

8 Paint a scene from the Harlem Renaissance.

9 Make a poster advertising a Louis Armstrong show from the Jazz Age.

10 Create a political cartoon about the Teapot Dome Scandal.

11 Examine political cartoons about Prohibition.

12 Make a poster about the political views of Marcus Garvey.

13 Create a PowerPoint about several inventions of Thomas Edison.

14 Watch the film *The Great Gatsby*.

Musical/Rhythmic

1 Listen to music from the Jazz Age.

2 Listen to five songs performed by Louis Armstrong.

3 Evaluate the music of Duke Ellington.

4 Perform the Charleston dance.

5 Learn about the instruments of the Jazz Age.

6 Determine the impact African music had on the Jazz Age.

7 Research the origin of swing music.

8 Learn about the dance halls of New York in the 1920s.

9 Sing a song from the Jazz Age as a duo.

10 Play, a popular song from the 1920s for the class.

Chapter 12 continued
The Roaring '20s
(1920–1929)

★ Bodily/Kinesthetic

1. Re-create the Scopes Monkey Trial.
2. Act out the role of Babe Ruth before a big baseball game.
3. Act out the concept, "flapper."
4. Create a project about the Harlem Renaissance.
5. Perform a dance from the 1920s.
6. Build a model of a famous landmark constructed in the 1920s.
7. Role-play a sports fan in the 1920s talking about his or her favorite sport.
8. Act out the role of President Harding after hearing about the Teapot Dome Scandal.
9. Perform a pantomime about Prohibition.
10. Role-play Charles Lindbergh after landing in France.
11. Build a puzzle about Presidents Warren Harding and Calvin Coolidge.
12. Perform a skit about the "Red Scare."

★ Naturalist

1. Record the changes in farming techniques in the 1920s that increased farm production.
2. Categorize the raw materials needed for Harvey Firestone's tires.
3. Record the changes in the automobile due to the refinement of gasoline.
4. List the natural materials used to make illegal bathroom gin during Prohibition.
5. Classify substances that were made illegal with the passage of the Volstead Act.
6. Identify the source or origin of Spanish Influenza, which killed over 500,000 Americans.
7. Record the changes in highway construction during the 1920s.
8. Observe pictures of oil rigs across Oklahoma. Describe them to a partner.
9. Observe changes in food production as a result of the research of George Washington Carver.
10. Using a graphic organizer, to show patterns of U.S. immigration in the 1920s.

Experience U.S. History! • Rickey Millwood
Kagan Publishing • 1 (800) 933-2667 • www.KaganOnline.com

Interpersonal

1 Debate the issue of Prohibition.

2 Write a collaborative paper on changes in transportation during the 1920s.

3 Do a team presentation about the Harlem Renaissance.

4 Interview each other about the passage of the 19th, or suffrage, Amendment.

5 Practice criticizing the Supreme Court case decision in the child labor case of *Hammer v. Daggenhart*.

6 Discuss with a partner the Palmer Raids and the Red Scare.

7 Share with others your opinion of the ruling in the Scopes Monkey Trial.

8 Interview each other about the poetry of Langston Hughes.

9 Do a team presentation on the Jazz Age.

10 Share with others the changing role of women in the 1920s.

Intrapersonal

1 Make an action plan to enforce Prohibition.

2 Write about the actions of Margaret Sanger.

3 Observe and discuss the change in morals during the roaring 20s.

4 Describe your feelings about Henry Ford.

5 Describe your feelings about the Palmer Raids.

6 Express your likes and dislikes about W. E. B. Dubois.

7 Defend this statement by President Calvin Coolidge: "The business of business is business."

8 Write about the actions of sports heroes in the 1920s.

9 Weigh alternatives to Prohibition.

10 Defend the 19th Amendment.

11 Write your feelings about the Civil Rights in the 1920s.

12 Weigh alternatives to the actions by Congress to restrict immigration in the 1920s.

Experience U.S. History! • Rickey Millwood

12.1 Blackline Master • Visual/Spatial Activity

The Roaring '20s

The Suffrage Movement

Women, excluded from voting in the 15th Amendment, now gained the right to vote with the passage of the 19th Amendment. Women could now express their political preferences and would play a major role in American politics in years to come.

World War I had provided the motive for women to demand the right to vote. Long overdue, women gained this privilege in 1920. Susan B. Anthony had led the way in this fight. Unfortunately, she died before the 19th Amendment went into effect. All American citizens owe her gratitude for her endurance and determination. Her strength truly exhibits what this great nation is about.

Instructions: Make a poster, as if the year were 1914, urging Congress to allow women to vote.

The Roaring '20s

The Scopes Monkey Trial

In 1925, a young biology teacher was placed on trial in Tennessee for teaching evolution in the public school system. Could the theories of Charles Darwin and evolution be taught in the Bible Belt?

This question was addressed in a famous case. The teacher was John Scopes and the court case that ensued is referred to as the Scopes Monkey Trial. Clarence Darrow represented Scopes, and William Jennings Bryan represented the state. Bryan even took the stand and was made to appear foolish after being questioned by Darrow. In fact, the trial took such a toll on Bryan that he died just shortly after the conclusion. The court upheld the law and ordered that Scopes pay a small fine. This hotly debated issue about evolution would continue for years to come.

EXTRA!! EXTRA!!

Instructions: Write a newspaper article about the trial of John Scopes.

12.3 Blackline Master • Musical/Rhythmic Activity

The Roaring '20s

The Harlem Renaissance

A revival of culture and art thrived in Harlem, New York, in the 1920s. Harlem became one of the largest African American communities in the nation. The Harlem Renaissance was a flowering of African American literature, art, music, and culture—all centered in one location. A major factor contributing to this was the large migration of African Americans from the South to northern cities. Through the 1920s and 1930s, Harlem was filled with talented individuals who expressed their great talent.

Instructions: Write a song about the Harlem Renaissance.

Experience U.S. History! • Rickey Millwood
Kagan Publishing • 1 (800) 933-2667 • www.KaganOnline.com

12.4 Blackline Master • Bodily/Kinesthetic Activities

The Roaring '20s

Transatlantic Aviation, a New Era of Travel

Flying through cold air and sleepy, Charles Lindbergh made a historical crossing of the Atlantic in 1927. Landing in France, he was received with a hero's welcome. His flight paved the avenue for the advancement of technology in the field of aviation which improved planes and long-distance flying. This flight was much more than a crossing of the ocean. Lindbergh, in his "Spirit of St. Louis" landing in Paris, was a symbol of American pride in the field of transportation. In the 1930s, female aviator Amelia Earhart would capture the imaginations of Americans—just as Lindbergh did years earlier in the 1920s.

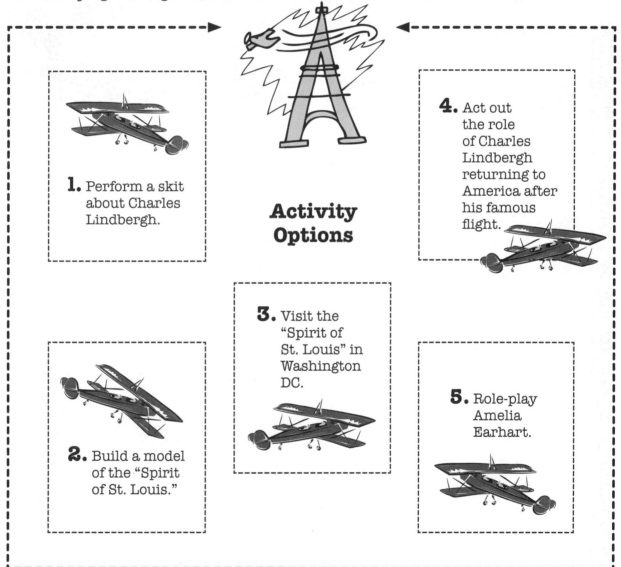

Activity Options

1. Perform a skit about Charles Lindbergh.

2. Build a model of the "Spirit of St. Louis."

3. Visit the "Spirit of St. Louis" in Washington DC.

4. Act out the role of Charles Lindbergh returning to America after his famous flight.

5. Role-play Amelia Earhart.

Chapter 13: The Great Depression (1929-1942)

The Great Depression began in America with the Stock Market Crash in 1929. That was only the beginning. Banks would close by the thousands and massive unemployment resulted. This period of gloom and despair did not fully end until America entered World War II. Many Americans blamed President Herbert Hoover for the Great Depression, therefore, they elected Franklin Roosevelt as president in 1932. America had confronted economic problems in the past but never of this magnitude. No story tells it better than Steinbeck's *The Grapes of Wrath*.

Verbal/Linguistic

1 Analyze the major causes of the Great Depression.

2 Create a word web about Herbert Hoover's economic policies.

3 Create a list of vocabulary terms associated with the Great Depression.

4 Read *The Grapes of Wrath*.

5 Create a crossword puzzle about the Stock Market Crash of 1929.

6 Write a paper about the closure of banks as a result of the Stock Market Crash.

7 Explain the concept of buying on margin.

8 Write a play about a family coping during the Great Depression.

9 Write a poem about the soup kitchens of the Great Depression.

10 Complete a descriptive writing exercise about life in the Dust Bowl region.

11 Form a plan that would have ended the Great Depression before 1942.

12 Evaluate the impact the Great Depression had on America.

Logical/Mathematical

1 Chart America's unemployment rate from 1929 to 1942.

2 Analyze patterns in the stock market for the month of October 1929.

3 Graph the number of bank failures between 1929 and 1932.

4 Determine how and why a major African American migration occurred during the Great Depression.

5 Compare and contrast the Great Depression with the Panic of 1837.

6 Analyze and organize the election data of 1932.

8 Sequence the major events of the Great Depression on a time line, beginning with the Stock Market Crash.

9 Calculate the probability of becoming unemployed during the Great Depression.

10 Estimate the number of Hoovervilles across America during the Great Depression.

11 Describe the impact of the Hawley Smoot Tariff during the Great Depression.

12 Determine the number of farm foreclosures during the Great Depression.

Visual/Spatial

1 Watch the film *The Grapes of Wrath*.

2 Create a map illustrating the Dust Bowl.

3 Draw a scene of the Stock Market Crash.

4 Create a political cartoon about Herbert Hoover's economic policies.

5 Create a skit about the unemployed during the Great Depression.

6 Examine photographs of the unemployed during the Great Depression.

7 Create a PowerPoint that illustrates the causes of the Great Depression.

8 Imagine and discuss life for African Americans during the Great Depression years.

9 View clips of Mary Pickford's movies.

10 Create a slogan about how the Great Depression affected Americans.

11 Examine and post in the classroom pictures of clothing worn in the 1930s.

12 Paint a picture of life in America during the 1930s.

13 Post pictures around the classroom of scenes from the Great Depression.

14 Find pictures of famous athletes during the 1930s. Compare and contrast their uniforms with those of today's athletes.

15 Locate pictures of new inventions from the Great Depression era. Describe the inventions to a partner.

Musical/Rhythmic

1 Listen to swing music by Duke Ellington.

2 Interpret the words to the song "Brother Can You Spare a Dime?"

3 Research the effect the Great Depression had on a famous American musician.

4 Play class songs or records from the Great Depression.

5 Listen to the music of Glenn Miller.

6 Learn about the instruments played in the big bands during the Great Depression era.

7 Examine and listen to the songs of Woodie Guthrie.

8 Create a collage of musical composers from the Great Depression era.

9 Write a song about the Great Depression.

10 Change the words to a popular song today and make it about the Great Depression.

11 Evaluate the impact of patriotic music during the 1930s.

12 Listen to the music of different genres during the Great Depression.

Experience U.S. History! • Rickey Millwood

Chapter 13 continued
The Great Depression
(1929–1942)

Bodily/Kinesthetic

1 Perform a skit about the Stock Market Crash.

2 Perform a play about stock investors on October 29, 1929.

3 Put together a typical meal eaten during the Great Depression era.

4 Act out the role of a farming family evicted from their farm in the Midwest.

5 Act out the role of a bank customer in line demanding his or her savings.

6 Role-play Herbert Hoover explaining his views toward the Great Depression.

7 Make a video about life during the Great Depression years.

8 Act out the role of a banker telling customers the bank has collapsed.

9 Role-play Franklin Roosevelt in the 1932 campaign.

10 Role-play an American observing Herbert Hoover leave the White House in 1933.

11 Role-play a hobo traveling across America during the Great Depression years.

12 Act out the role of a Hollywood star during the 1930s.

13 Build a model of a famous structure from the 1930s.

Naturalist

1 Determine the ecological causes of the American Dust Bowl.

2 Record changes in rainfall levels in the Midwest in the early 1930s that contributed to the Dust Bowl.

3 Categorize the materials used to build shanty towns.

4 List the characteristics of a Hooverville.

5 Visit any building constructed during the Great Depression years.

6 Categorize changes in clothing materials during the Great Depression.

7 Visit or observe on the Internet the Hoover Dam in Colorado.

8 Determine how the Great Depression affected America's livestock supply.

9 Record changes in crop production from 1929 until 1932.

10 Note changes in road construction from 1929 until 1932.

11 Discover changes in forestry practices during the Great Depression years.

12 Create a log of several laws that dealt with pollution or toxic waste during the Great Depression.

13 Determine the impact the boll weevil had on the nation's cotton crop during the 1930s.

Experience U.S. History! • Rickey Millwood
Kagan Publishing • 1 (800) 933-2667 • www.KaganOnline.com

Interpersonal

1 Discuss with a partner Herbert Hoover's economic policies toward ending the Great Depression.

2 Criticize the bank failures.

3 Do a team presentation on the issues in the 1932 election.

4 Share with others your ideas on why the Great Depression lasted so long.

5 Tutor a classmate in understanding the operation of the stock market.

6 Write a collaborative paper on the causes of the Great Depression.

7 Take turns stating the most difficult aspects of the Great Depression.

8 Do a team presentation on the conditions in the Dust Bowl.

9 Interview each other about the differences between Herbert Hoover and Franklin Roosevelt.

10 Reach a consensus on why Herbert Hoover unleashed the military on the Bonus Army.

11 Share with others ideas about education during the Great Depression years.

12 Plan an event on October 29 to remember the Stock Market Crash.

Intrapersonal

1 Choose between using revenue from the government or a private charity to combat the Great Depression. Explain your choice in writing.

2 Make an action plan that would have prevented the banks from closing.

3 Meditate on life during the Great Depression for females and African Americans. Share your feelings with a partner.

4 Write about the needs of children during the Great Depression.

5 Express your opinion on Herbert Hoover's brutal attack on the Bonus Army.

6 Observe and discuss mood changes in Americans from the early 1920s to the early 1930s.

7 Express your likes and dislikes about Herbert Hoover.

8 Defend the position by Herbert Hoover to allow private charities to take care of the nation.

9 Relate the devastation from the Dust Bowl to the devastation from hurricanes in 2005.

10 Take a stance to elect Franklin Roosevelt as president in 1932.

11 Write a personal poem about life during the Great Depression.

12 Make an action plan to prevent the stock market from collapsing again.

13 Critique any movie or book about the Great Depression.

14 Respond to the hypothetical dilemma of another Great Depression.

13.1 Blackline Master • Intrapersonal Activity

The Great Depression

The Nation Faces Depression

Often seen rambling through landfills, unemployed and homeless Americans desperately searched for food. America had seen some tough economic times in its past—but nothing of this magnitude. The Great Depression began in 1929 and would last 13 long bitter years. Close to 25 percent of the nation was unemployed by 1933. The high rate of unemployment strangled the nation until the coming of World War II. Women and African Americans especially suffered during this period. Men that had provided for their families now felt helpless.

Most of the nation blamed Herbert Hoover for the Great Depression. But it's too easy to blame one individual for this event. The nation held him responsible, however, and in 1932 Hoover would be defeated by Franklin Roosevelt. President Roosevelt's New Deal had many positive effects but there was no quick fix to this economic disaster. It would take America's entry into World War II to end the Great Depression.

Instructions: Imagine you lived in the early 1930s. Describe your feelings about thousands of banks collapsing and your savings accounts being completely wiped out.

Experience U.S. History! • Rickey Millwood
Kagan Publishing • 1 (800) 933-2667 • www.KaganOnline.com

13.2 Blackline Master • Logical/Mathematical Activity

The Great Depression

The Numbers Tell the Story

The 1920s, were prosperous times but the crash of the stock market in 1929 devastated the nation. Millions became unemployed and banks went broke by the thousands. Imagine losing your job and all of your money in the bank in one day. An economic blizzard swept quickly across America.

Remember, money in the bank was not insured at this time. People lined up at banks and demanded their savings—but there was no money left. Banks had loaned out money, and now the money was gone forever.

The American people had faced tough times in the past, but nothing like this. Now, Americans would go hungry and beg for food and jobs.

A somber mood settled over the nation but in 1932 Franklin Roosevelt offered hope. Millions had voted for him as he promised a New Deal. Roosevelt's Fireside Chats offered words of encouragement and hope over the radio, but the nation would not fully pull out of this Great Depression until the coming of World War II.

Instructions: Chart the rate of unemployment in America from 1929 until 1940.

1929 1930 1931 1932 1933 1934 1935 1936 1937 1938 1939 1940

Experience U.S. History! • Rickey Millwood
Kagan Publishing • 1 (800) 933-2667 • www.KaganOnline.com

The Great Depression

The Dust Bowl

Clouds of dust swirling through the air for miles were seen across the Great Plains in 1934. The central part of the nation would now face the Great Depression due to weather conditions and farming practices. No rain for months caused severe drought from Texas to southern Nebraska. Agricultural practices had torn the soil loose, and dust storms circulated through the entire region.

The dust storms lasted for days and covered entire towns. Banks foreclosed farms where bills were not paid. Farmers lost their land and were forced to move in massive numbers.

Various causes have contributed to American migration—this time weather was the contributing factor. Gold had lured settlers to the West in the 1840s and now the search for a job would pull thousands to the West. People left the central region desperately seeking employment. These immigrants were not welcome in the West. They were seen as intruders and not as fellow Americans. The West offered little hope. This Great Depression completely covered the nation and no region would escape it.

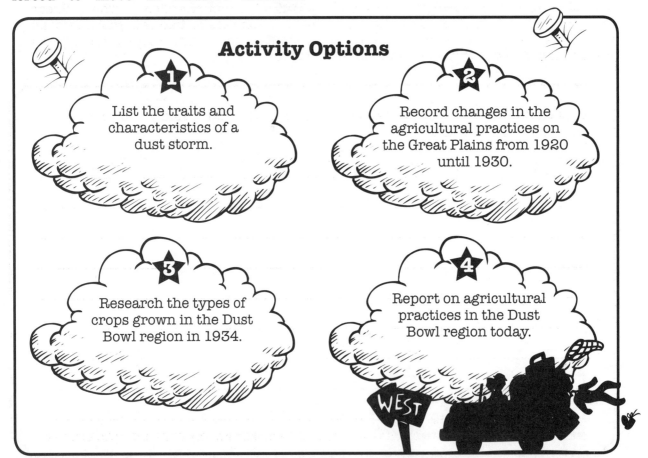

Activity Options

1. List the traits and characteristics of a dust storm.
2. Record changes in the agricultural practices on the Great Plains from 1920 until 1930.
3. Research the types of crops grown in the Dust Bowl region in 1934.
4. Report on agricultural practices in the Dust Bowl region today.

13.4 Blackline Master • Verbal/Linguistic Activity

The Great Depression

Firing on the Bonus Army

Veterans from World War I watched in horror as President Hoover unleashed the Army on them in 1932. Why would the Army attack its own veterans?

In the summer of 1932, about 20,000 World War I veterans went to Washington DC and demanded their pensions early. Led by Walter Waters, these veterans demanded the pensions they were promised. The Great Depression caused the veterans to demand the bonuses earlier than promised.

President Hoover had no intention of allowing these protestors to stay in Washington DC. So, a fight broke out between police and the Bonus Army. Two veterans were killed by the police, but the veterans fought back. President Hoover then decided to send in federal troops to attack the veterans. The Army used tear gas and torches to destroy the camps the veterans had erected. Even children in the area were gassed.

Ordered to break up the Bonus Army, General MacArthur used rough tactics against former American soldiers to drive them out of Washington DC. The veterans returned home empty-handed. The Great Depression had caused Americans to fight against Americans in the nation's capital.

Instructions: Write a newspaper article about the Bonus Army and their march on Washington DC.

EXTRA!!EXTRA!!EXTRA!!EXTRA!!EXTRA!!EXTRA!!EXTRA!!EXTRA!!EXTRA!!

Experience U.S. History! • Rickey Millwood
Kagan Publishing • 1 (800) 933-2667 • www.KaganOnline.com

Chapter 14
Roosevelt's New Deal
(1932-1945)

President Franklin Roosevelt gave the American people hope through the Great Depression with his New Deal programs. Americans listened to the president as he soothed their fears with his Fireside Chats. The New Deal programs did not take America out of the Depression completely, but the programs did offer employment and opportunity to thousands of desperate Americans. The nation loved President Roosevelt and elected him four times. He would soon lead the country through World War II.

Verbal/Linguistic

1 Discuss the concept of a "New Deal" during the Great Depression years.

2 Write a persuasive paper about the need for employment programs such as the Public Works Administration.

3 Make a word web about the New Deal programs.

4 Write a poem about Roosevelt's court-packing scheme.

5 Debate the concept of the Social Security program.

6 Complete a creative writing exercise about the 1932 election.

7 Compare and contrast the economic views of Presidents Hoover and Roosevelt.

8 Explain the New Deal phrase "priming the pump."

9 Give examples of the phrase "Relief, Recovery, and Reform."

10 Write a skit about the Fireside Chats.

11 Write a newspaper story about Roosevelt's first 100 days as president.

12 Share ideas about the success or failure of the New Deal programs.

Logical/Mathematical

1 Graph unemployment figures from 1929 to 1942.

2 Determine the years the New Deal had the greatest impact on easing unemployment.

3 Determine the number of unemployed women in 1932.

4 Determine the cost of one New Deal program.

5 Find the amount of Social Security a wage earner paid into the system in 1946.

7 Calculate the number of Tennessee Valley Authority (TVA) dams built and the hydroelectric power produced.

8 Discover patterns of employment and migration in regions where the TVA constructed dams.

9 Sequence the events on a time line of New Deal legislation.

10 Use inductive reasoning to determine President Roosevelt's popularity.

11 Analyze data that proves the New Deal programs were successful in reducing unemployment.

12 Synthesize ideas about programs America needs today.

Experience U.S. History! • Rickey Millwood
Kagan Publishing • 1 (800) 933-2667 • www.KaganOnline.com

⭐ Visual/Spatial ⭐

1 Make a PowerPoint presentation of the New Deal programs.

2 Create a chart that shows an increase in employment as a result of the New Deal programs.

3 Create a logo about Roosevelt's Social Security program.

4 Draw a scene of Americans employed in one New Deal program.

5 Create a graphic organizer of all New Deal programs that involve banking practices.

6 Draw a political cartoon of the "Bank Holiday."

7 Create a political cartoon of the opponents of the New Deal.

8 Create a political cartoon of Roosevelt's court-packing scheme.

9 Design a crossword puzzle of the New Deal Programs.

10 Examine a map of the 1936 presidential election results.

11 Create a map that shows the location of the TVA dams.

12 Paint or draw a scene of everyday life under the Roosevelt administration.

⭐ Musical/Rhythmic ⭐

1 Determine the top 10 record hits during the 1930s.

2 Listen to the sound track of a popular 1930s movie.

3 Listen to the lyrics of the "Lullaby of Broadway."

4 Listen to President Roosevelt's campaign song, "Happy Days Are Here Again."

5 Perform a popular dance before the class from the 1930s or 1940s.

6 Perform a concert on popular songs from the Roosevelt years.

7 Compose a song about the New Deal programs and write it to the tune of a popular song today.

8 Research a music composer during the 1930s or 1940s.

9 Learn about the changes in any musical instruments or sounds during the early 1940s.

10 Evaluate the music people listened to during the New Deal years.

Experience U.S. History! • Rickey Millwood
Kagan Publishing • 1 (800) 933-2667 • www.KaganOnline.com

Chapter 14 continued
Roosevelt's New Deal
(1932–1945)

⭐ Bodily/Kinesthetic

1 Act out President Roosevelt giving a Fire-side Chat.

2 Perform a skit about a Civilian Conservation Corps (CCC) employee.

3 Role-play an opponent of the Civil Works Administration.

4 Perform a skit about Roosevelt's court-packing scheme.

5 Build a model of a TVA dam.

6 Learn about polio and its affect on President Roosevelt.

7 Role-play any member of Roosevelt's Brain Trust.

8 Act out the role of an artist that joined the Works Progress Administration.

9 Give a speech as Alf Landon in the 1936 campaign against President Roosevelt.

10 Act out the role of Senator Huey "Kingfish" Long, advocating relief for the poor.

⭐ Naturalist

1 Record changes in the Dust Bowl region after the New Deal went into effect.

2 List the characteristics of the Tennessee Valley before the creation of the TVA.

3 Record the developmental stages of dams in the Tennessee Valley after 1933.

4 Capture with a camera or view on the Internet a picture of a TVA dam.

5 Categorize the major responsibilities of the CCC.

6 Categorize items or badges given to CCC members.

7 Record changes in farming practices as a result of the Agricultural Adjustment Act.

8 List the responsibilities of an employee of the Civil Works Administration.

9 Examine and discuss President Roosevelt's views of national parks.

10 Research President Roosevelt's policy toward the reservation system in the Great Plains region.

Experience U.S. History! • **Rickey Millwood**
Kagan Publishing • 1 (800) 933-2667 • www.KaganOnline.com

Interpersonal

1 Discuss with a partner one New Deal program that you feel had the greatest impact during the Depression.

2 Interview each other about the New Deal programs.

3 Divide the class in teams. Have each team do a presentation on a different New Deal program.

4 Discuss with a partner the major goals of President Roosevelt during the Great Depression years.

5 Criticize a wasteful New Deal program.

6 Reach a consensus on the impact of youth involvement in the CCC.

7 Role-play Congressional officials and mediate the conflict over court-packing.

8 Practice active listening to the Fireside Chats.

9 Solve problems as a team that women faced during the Great Depression years.

10 Share with others the change in voting habits by African Americans as a result of Roosevelt's presidency.

11 Discuss with a partner how African Americans broke with the Republicans as a result of the Great Depression.

12 Do a team presentation on the Indian Reorganization Act.

Intrapersonal

1 Express your likes and dislikes about President Franklin Roosevelt.

2 Weigh alternatives to the New Deal.

3 Defend the decision by President Roosevelt to court-pack the Supreme Court.

4 Describe your feelings about the current Social Security system.

5 List the priorities you feel should have been implemented immediately in 1933.

6 Observe and describe changes in unemployment by 1936 as a result of the New Deal programs.

7 Assume you had been elected president during the Great Depression. Form an action plan to get America out of the Great Depression.

8 Write about the actions of President Roosevelt in confronting the Great Depression.

9 Defend the position by African Americans to migrate to the North during the Great Depression years.

10 Defend President Roosevelt's actions during his first 100 days in office.

Experience U.S. History! • Rickey Millwood
Kagan Publishing • 1 (800) 933-2667 • www.KaganOnline.com

14.1 Blackline Master • Naturalist Activities

Roosevelt's New Deal

The Tennessee Valley Project

Residents living along the Tennessee River faced constant threats of floods. Flooding through Tennessee and Alabama was common due to the massive Tennessee River. This region was one of the poorest in the nation, but that was about to change as a result of the New Deal. The TVA drastically transformed this region into an area that would attract people.

The government changed this area with a plan that called for the building of massive dams to control the Tennessee River. These dams could control flooding and provide hydroelectric power. The construction of these dams provided many jobs and more importantly, helped develop an impoverished region.

The TVA was a tremendous success. In fact, it could be argued that it had more success than any other New Deal program. This region now provides electricity from dams, but people also enjoy recreation on these reservoirs.

Activity Options

1. View pictures on the internet of a TVA dam and write a description of it.

2. List the characteristics of the Tennessee Valley before dams were constructed.

3. Describe the steps in building a massive TVA dam.

4. Visit a TVA dam or lake.

5. Record the changes in life in the Tennessee Valley after the project was completed.

Experience U.S. History! • Rickey Millwood
Kagan Publishing • 1 (800) 933-2667 • www.KaganOnline.com

Roosevelt's New Deal

Social Security

For many Americans, Social Security is their only source of income. How did this program begin? Why is this program considered the most controversial of all the New Deal programs? What does the future hold for Social Security?

This program was actually in the second phase of the New Deal. The program was established in 1935; the intent was to provide an income for individuals over 65. It was also set up to assist dependents and individuals who were handicapped.

Today, Social Security is in serious financial trouble. Recent changes have increased the retirement age and Social Security taxes are now expensive. These measures are being applied in an attempt to save the system. Many workers feel they will never receive the benefits for their contributions. They feel the system may collapse before they ever reach retirement.

The federal government feels the system is currently sound but may go broke unless measures are taken. However, most politicians fear changes in the system. Therefore, Social Security is still the one program from the New Deal that is hotly debated in Congress.

Instructions: Calculate the average Social Security monthly income.

Roosevelt's New Deal

The Alphabet Soup Programs

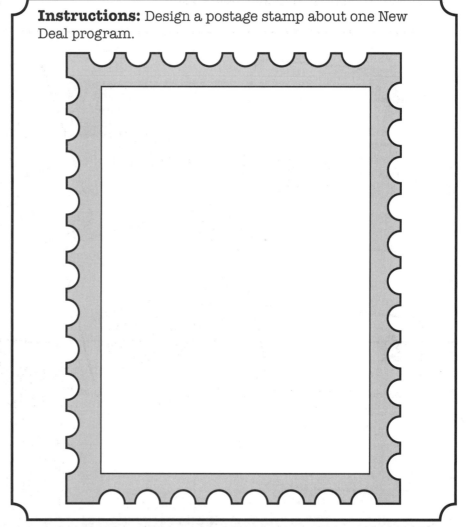

The New Deal programs flooded out of Washington DC during the first 100 days of the Roosevelt administration. These programs had many intentions, and some were more successful than others. President Roosevelt had promised Americans relief, recovery, and reform, and he meant to deliver on that promise.

Sometimes, he ran into opposition with the Supreme Court. The president was able to establish many controversial programs, but changing the Constitution was another matter. President Roosevelt decided that if he could place six additional judges on the Supreme Court, he could keep all his New Deal legislation from being struck down.

This scheme to increase the Supreme Court to 15 justices was known as court-packing. Roosevelt stated that it was time to add some new blood to the court, but his true intention was to have a majority of judges on his side. Americans did not want their Supreme Court tampered with—not even by Franklin Roosevelt. The three branches of government were too sacred to be changed.

Thus the plan to add six justices backfired. The Supreme Court did strike down some New Deal programs such as the National Recovery Act, but we still have some of the programs today.

Instructions: Design a postage stamp about one New Deal program.

14.4 Blackline Master • Bodily/Kinesthetic Activities

Roosevelt's New Deal

The Fireside Chats

The American people felt betrayed by President Hoover during the Great Depression and voted him out of office in 1932. There was tremendous confidence in newly elected President Roosevelt (FDR). The new president kept in touch with the nation through radio talks. Through the years of his presidency, he informed the nation of a wide range of topics in at least 28 speeches. He spoke on subjects such as banks, New Deal programs, adding judges to the Supreme Court, and war with Japan.

The Fireside Chats calmed fears in Americans and gave the nation hope during grim times. These radio programs restored confidence in Americans because the president was keeping them informed about our nation. The nation loved FDR perhaps more than any other president and elected him four times.

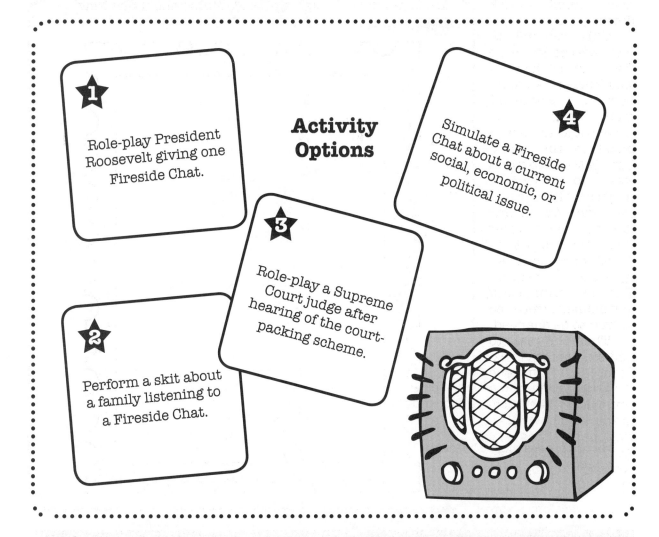

Activity Options

1. Role-play President Roosevelt giving one Fireside Chat.

2. Perform a skit about a family listening to a Fireside Chat.

3. Role-play a Supreme Court judge after hearing of the court-packing scheme.

4. Simulate a Fireside Chat about a current social, economic, or political issue.

Experience U.S. History! • Rickey Millwood
Kagan Publishing • 1 (800) 933-2667 • www.KaganOnline.com

Chapter 15
World War II and the Holocaust
(1939–1945)

The devastating attack at Pearl Harbor on December 7, 1941, instantly brought the United States into World War II. The nation would fight the Axis powers and defeat all three by 1945. The conclusion of World War II would come with the dropping of two atomic bombs on Japan and the releasing of victims in concentration camps across Europe. Horrific atrocities were discovered at these sites. The Holocaust revealed crimes on a scale never before witnessed in human history.

Verbal/Linguistic

1 Write a persuasive argument for America's entry into World War II after the attack at Pearl Harbor.

2 Compare and contrast the feeling about war in America before and after the attack at Pearl Harbor.

3 Discuss the Holocaust.

4 Share ideas about how World War II took America out of the Great Depression.

5 Write a report on the role American women played in industrial output in World War II.

6 Compare the attack at Pearl Harbor with the attack on 9-11.

7 Write a newspaper article about American soldiers entering concentration camps as liberators.

8 Discuss the results of the Yalta Conference.

9 Read about President Truman's decision to drop two atomic bombs on Japan.

10 Write a paper supporting or condemning the use of atomic weapons on Hiroshima and Nagasaki.

Logical/Mathematical

1 Brainstorm ideas about America's preparation for entry into World War II.

2 List and organize facts about the Holocaust.

3 Categorize rationed items during the war.

4 Sequence the major events of World War II on a time line, beginning with Germany's attack on Poland in 1939.

5 Graph patterns of migration during the war.

6 Graph the number of American causalities during the years 1941–1945.

7 Calculate in dollars the cost of World War II.

8 Calculate the loss of life and damage inflicted on Hiroshima and Nagasaki.

9 Compare and contrast the European and Pacific theaters of war.

10 Use reasoning to determine why new cars were not built during World War II.

11 Evaluate the ideas of President Roosevelt at the Yalta Conference.

12 Graph the damage inflicted by kamikaze planes from 1942–1945.

Experience U.S. History! • Rickey Millwood
Kagan Publishing • 1 (800) 933-2667 • www.KaganOnline.com

Visual/Spatial

1 View the film *Tora Tora Tora*.

2 View the film *Pearl Harbor*.

3 View the film *Escape from Sobibor*.

4 View the film *The Sands of Iwo Jima*.

5 Examine photographs of Hiroshima and Nagasaki after atomic bombs were dropped.

6 View a film of the liberation of the concentration camps at the end of the Holocaust.

7 Watch the film *The Devil's Arithmetic*.

8 Make a PowerPoint about kamikaze planes used by Japan in World War II.

9 Draw a scene of the Japanese-American interment camps.

10 Draw a scene of women contributing to the war effort on the home front.

11 Draw a political cartoon about America's entry into World War II.

12 Create a PowerPoint about the major world leaders in World War II.

Musical/Rhythmic

1 Determine how music boosted the morale of soldiers in World War II.

2 Identify the songs of the early 1940s that were top hits on the charts.

3 Listen to the sound of the big bands of the early 1940s.

4 Listen to the tune "Boogie Woogie Bugle Boy from Company B."

5 Listen and interpret the lyrics to "Remember Pearl Harbor."

6 Compare the music of World War I to the music of World War II.

7 Listen to and interpret the song "Der Fuehrer's jace."

8 Write a song about a major event in World War II and put it to the tune of a popular song you know.

9 Play a popular song from World War II for the class.

10 Evaluate the music from the 1940s.

11 Listen to music from the various nations involved in World War II.

12 Create a list of the top 10 songs during World War II.

Chapter 15 continued
World War II and the Holocaust
(1939-1945)

Bodily/Kinesthetic

1 Role-play President Roosevelt in his speech after the attack on Pearl Harbor.

2 Perform a skit about women working in factories during World War II.

3 Act out the role of a Holocaust survivor in World War II.

4 Visit a World War II battlefield or museum.

5 Build or assemble a small model of a plane or tank used in World War II.

6 Act out the role of an American citizen after hearing of the attack at Pearl Harbor.

7 Interview a soldier that served in World War II.

8 Design a puzzle about the major battles in World War II.

9 Interview a woman that worked in a factory during World War II.

10 Role-play an American POW from World War II.

11 Do a pantomime about survivors from Pearl Harbor or Hiroshima.

12 Perform a skit about the end of World War II.

Naturalist

1 Visit a Holocaust museum.

2 View on the Internet or visit the statue of the Iwo Jima Monument.

3 Visit the battleship *North Carolina* in Wilmington, North Carolina.

4 Visit a World War II memorial.

5 Determine the weather at Pearl Harbor on December 7, 1941.

6 Watch a video or examine the beaches where American soldiers landed on D-Day.

7 View pictures of the atomic bomb tests in New Mexico.

8 Determine the impact the weather played in the historic Battle of the Bulge.

9 Show and discuss a picture of a "Victory Garden."

10 Visit a military base established on a Pacific island during World War II.

11 Visit historical Warm Springs, Georgia.

12 View pictures of Hiroshima and Nagasaki after atomic bombs were dropped. Describe your feelings to a partner.

Experience U.S. History! • Rickey Millwood
Kagan Publishing • 1 (800) 933-2667 • www.KaganOnline.com

Interpersonal

1 Interview each other about America's greatest challenges of entering World War II.

2 Share with others your opinion about how World War II changed America forever.

3 Write a paper explaining why the United States did not stop the Holocaust until 1945.

4 Discuss with a partner the shock that Pearl Harbor had upon the nation.

5 Debate the issue to defeat Nazi Germany before defeating Japan.

6 Do a team presentation on the concentration camps of the Third Reich.

7 Do a team presentation on key battles of World War II.

8 Reach a consensus on conducting the Manhattan Project in New Mexico.

9 Interview each other about the dropping of atomic bombs on August 6 and August 9, 1945.

10 Role-play the crew of the "Enola Gay" after dropping the atomic bomb on Hiroshima.

11 Create a plan to deal with shortages caused by World War II.

12 Interview a Holocaust survivor.

13 Role-play Harry Truman defending the use of the atomic bomb.

14 Plan an event around Veterans or Memorial Day.

Intrapersonal

1 Defend America's position to stay out of World War II until 1941.

2 Express your feelings about the placement of Japanese Americans in internment camps during World War II.

3 Prioritize the major goals of preparing the nation for World War II.

4 Make an action plan for defeating Nazi, Germany.

5 Observe and describe the mood changes in Hitler and Mussolini by 1944.

6 Think about the actions of Dr. Robert Oppenheimer in heading up the Manhattan Project. Share your thoughts with a partner.

7 Weigh alternatives to stopping the Holocaust.

8 Take a stance either for or against dropping two atomic bombs on Japan.

9 Write about the actions of Harry Truman in deciding to drop two atomic bombs.

10 Defend the position to create a United Nations at the end World War II.

11 Write about the needs of American citizens during World War II.

12 Write a personal poem about the Holocaust.

13 Write an ethical code of behavior toward POWs during World War II.

14 Defend the policy to place war criminals on trial at the conclusion of the war.

15.1 **Blackline Master • Verbal/Linguistic Activity**

World War II and the Holocaust

The Attack at Pearl Harbor

December 7, 1941, was a day that will be forever remembered in American history—Japan attacked American forces at Pearl Harbor, Hawaii. The attack was well planned and delivered a devastating blow to American forces. The entire fleet of battleships suffered heavy damage and over 2,000 Americans died that Sunday morning.

In this surprise attack, Japan had hoped to deliver a punch so devastating to America that it could take control of the entire Pacific region. America had stayed out of World War II but would now enter the conflict against the Axis powers. President Roosevelt called it "a day that would live in infamy."

Instructions: Write a descriptive account as if you had witnessed the attack at Pearl Harbor.

15.2 **Blackline Master • Intrapersonal Activity**

World War II and the Holocaust

The Fate of the *St. Louis*

Imagine being on a ship and making it all the way across the Atlantic only to be sent back to Europe. Such was the case for the passengers on the *St. Louis*. This ship carried more than 900 passengers that were escaping Hitler's attack on Europe. Most of the passengers were Jews. The passengers hoped that they would be admitted to Cuba or the United States as refugees. Cuba refused to take these people and President Roosevelt denied them entry as well.

The United States was still in the Great Depression and there was an anti-immigrant mood across the country. The nation had already met its quota for immigrants. Workers out of jobs didn't want to compete with foreign labor. President Roosevelt simply refused to respond to telegrams from the ship, so the ship returned to Europe.

Many of these passengers were taken captive after they returned to Europe and died in the Holocaust. These refugees were so close to freedom but yet were turned away. The movie *Voyage of the Damned* reflects this tragic story.

Instructions: Express your likes and dislikes about the immigration policy during World War II.

Likes

Dislikes

Experience U.S. History! • Rickey Millwood
Kagan Publishing • 1 (800) 933-2667 • www.KaganOnline.com

123

World War II and the Holocaust

The Holocaust Begins

In November 1938, the Nazis attacked Jews all over Germany. Jews were beaten and arrested and their shops were looted. Jewish synagogues were then torched. This was called the Night of Broken Glass. Many people believe this event was the beginning of the Holocaust.

Adolf Hitler had picked on the Jews during his first five years in power, but this was open warfare. Concentration camps like Dachau would open. Soon, killing centers in Poland would exterminate millions in what Hitler called his Final Solution.

The U.S. government did know the Holocaust was happening, but the main goal when America did entered the war was to defeat Hitler's army. Over twelve million innocent people died in the Holocaust, including six million Jews.

It was hard for the world to believe this horrible event happened. Yet, it was very real and was documented on film. American soldiers were shocked as they liberated camps. Many of these camps were left standing as a reminder of the Holocaust.

Instructions: Design a book cover about the Holocaust.

15.4 Blackline Master • Logical/Mathematical Activity

World War II and the Holocaust

The Atomic Bombs

Japan refused to surrender during World War II even though Germany and Italy had been defeated. Japan would now face atomic destruction. Hiroshima and Nagasaki were—to be totally annihilated on August 6 and August 9, 1945. These cities were both targets for America's newest weapon, the atomic bomb. The world had never before seen such an awesome weapon. These bombs were equal to 20,000 tons of TNT. The damage was catastrophic and the loss of life horrific in both cities.

President Truman had authorized the use of these atomic weapons to save American lives and put an immediate end to the war. Both of those goals were achieved. These new weapons, which were built as a result of the Manhattan Project, ushered in the Atomic Age. Four years later, the Soviet Union exploded an atomic bomb and the Nuclear Arms Race began.

Instructions: Contrast the two atomic bombs.

Hiroshima

_____
_____
_____
_____
_____
_____
_____
_____
_____
_____

Nagasaki

_____
_____
_____
_____
_____
_____
_____
_____
_____
_____

Experience U.S. History! • Rickey Millwood
Kagan Publishing • 1 (800) 933-2667 • www.KaganOnline.com

Chapter 16: Living Through the Early Cold War Years (1945-1969)

The Cold War years are defined by the intense rivalry between the free and Communist worlds. The hostility between the United States and the Soviet Union began at the conclusion of World War II and did not end until the 1990s. During these years, the super-powers engaged in numerous global confrontations. The Cuban Missile Crisis, the most serious of all, nearly brought the two nations into nuclear war. During this period of the Cold War, the United States and the Soviet Union built up tens of thousands of nuclear missiles and warheads. Students in schools across America constantly practiced nuclear war drills.

Verbal/Linguistic

1 Analyze the phrase *Cold War*.

2 Read aloud the Iron Curtain Speech by Winston Churchill.

4 Write a research paper about the Marshall Plan or Truman Doctrine.

5 Write a poem about the Sputnik satellite.

6 Compare and contrast early American and Soviet space programs.

7 Create a word web of the "Cold War."

8 Complete a descriptive writing exercise about the Berlin Blockade.

9 Discuss the policy of containment and America's entry into the Korean Conflict.

10 Read about and discuss the construction of the Berlin Wall.

11 Debate the decisions made by President Kennedy during the Cuban Missile Crisis.

12 Write a newspaper article about the Cuban Missile Crisis.

13 Write a journal entry as Neil Armstrong about landing on the moon in July 1969.

Logical/Mathematical

1 Analyze financial data about the Marshall Plan.

2 Graph American lives lost in the Korean Conflict.

3 Chart how the Cold War affected America's defense budget from 1945 to 1969.

5 Compare and contrast the atomic bomb and the hydrogen bomb.

6 Determine why a nuclear arms race developed between the United States and Soviet Union.

7 Sequence the major events of the Cold War from 1945 to 1969 on a time line.

8 Evaluate the theory of stockpiling nuclear, chemical, and biological weapons during the Cold War to prevent another World War.

9 Evaluate President Kennedy's assassination conspiracy theories.

10 Compare and contrast the military strength of NATO and the Warsaw Pacts by 1969.

11 Contrast America's involvement in Korea and Vietnam.

12 List the effect the Sputnik satellite had on America.

Experience U.S. History! • Rickey Millwood
Kagan Publishing • 1 (800) 933-2667 • www.KaganOnline.com

★ Visual/Spatial ★

1 Design a map of Europe after 1945.

2 Create a political cartoon about the Berlin Blockade.

3 Watch a video about the construction of the Berlin Wall.

4 Create a political cartoon of General MacArthur's dismissal by President Truman.

5 Watch a video clip of any popular television show from the 1950s.

6 Find pictures of clothing worn in the 1950s.

7 Design a postcard about a major event in the 1950s.

8 Build a model of the Sputnik.

9 Design a political cartoon about the Berlin Wall.

10 Design a political cartoon about the Cuban Missile Crisis.

11 Make a poster about five popular movies during the 1950s or 1960s.

12 Draw a scene about America's landing on the moon.

13 Create a PowerPoint about new appliances built in the 1950s.

14 Examine photographs of automobiles made in the 1950s and 1960s.

15 Create a crossword puzzle about the major events of the Cold War.

★ Musical/Rhythmic ★

1 Examine the history of rock and roll music.

2 View a video of Elvis Presley on the *Ed Sullivan Show*.

3 Listen to the music of Diana Ross and the Supremes.

4 Watch a video clip of the Beatles' arrival in America.

5 Report on the music composed by African Americans during the 1950s.

6 Discover the African American writers and performers of rock and roll.

7 Discover patterns across America toward rock and roll music.

8 Listen to folk music of the 1960s.

9 Compare and contrast music from the 1950s and 1960s.

10 Listen to the music of Chuck Berry.

11 Listen to the music of Ray Charles.

12 Listen to the music of The Four Tops.

13 Identify five popular female singers from the 1950s and 1960s.

14 Interpret the lyrics to any novelty song from the 1950s or 1960s.

15 Listen to the music of The Temptations.

16 Identify a song from the 1950s or 1960s that refers to a major event.

Experience U.S. History! • Rickey Millwood

Chapter 16 continued
Living Through the Early Cold War Years
(1945-1969)

⭐ Bodily/Kinesthetic

1 Imitate the moves of Elvis Presley during the golden age of Rock n' Roll.

2 Perform the dance called the Twist by Chubby Checker.

3 Act out the role of a 1950s teen using a Hula hoop.

4 Perform a pantomime about the Cold War.

5 Build a model of the Berlin Wall.

6 Build a model of a spaceship from the 1960s.

7 Choreograph a re-enactment of Neil Armstrong's moon walk.

8 Act out the role of President Kennedy during the Cuban Missile Crisis.

9 Perform a skit about the Cuban Missile Crisis.

10 Create a puzzle about President Kennedy's assassination.

⭐ Naturalist

1 Research the reasons why President Eisenhower desired an interstate highway system across America.

2 Describe how the interstate highway systems changed America.

3 Create a map of the United States, showing all the interstate highways.

4 Find pictures of the first moon walk and determine the mineral composition of moon rocks.

5 Locate photographs of the physical features of the moon. Describe the features to a partner.

6 Record changes in America's space program from 1960 to 1969.

7 Visit the NASA Space Center in Florida.

8 Visit the Air and Space Museum in Washington DC.

9 Locate and write a poem about a picture of Earth made from outer space.

10 Record changes in space technology from 1960–1969.

11 Categorize the foods taken into space by astronauts.

12 Categorize the parts of a space suit.

13 Locate and discuss pictures of a nuclear power plant constructed during the Cold War.

14 Find and describe pictures of America's Intercontinental Ballistic Missiles (ICBMs) that were placed in silos in the desert soil during the Cold War.

15 Observe video of hydrogen bomb tests in Operation Crossroads.

16 View video of astronauts being extracted from the ocean after returning from outer space.

Experience U.S. History! • Rickey Millwood
Kagan Publishing • 1 (800) 933-2667 • www.KaganOnline.com

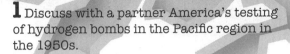

Interpersonal

1 Discuss with a partner America's testing of hydrogen bombs in the Pacific region in the 1950s.

2 Either praise or criticize both America and the Soviet Union for a nuclear arms race.

3 Interview each other about the roots of the Cold War.

4 Debate the issue of President Kennedy's handling of the Cuban Missile Crisis.

5 Take turns stating how life changed for American women in the 1950s.

6 Discuss with others the impact that *Brown v. Board of Education* would have upon America.

7 Do a team presentation on how music changed during the 1950s.

8 Write a term paper on the impact The Beatles had on America.

9 Solve the problem of financing and constructing the interstate highway system across America.

10 Discuss with a partner how the automobile industry changed in the 1950s.

11 Role-play member countries of the United Nations during the Cuban Missile Crisis.

12 Interview each other about the policy on Containment and the Domino Theory.

13 Reach a consensus about any conspiracy theory related to President Kennedy's death.

14 Do a team presentation on the construction of bomb or fallout shelters during the Cold War.

15 Take turns role-playing historical persons from the 1950s or 1960s before the class.

Intrapersonal

1 Prioritize America's major goals during the Cold War.

2 Describe your feelings about the construction of the Berlin Wall.

3 Describe your feelings about the way the Cuban Missile Crisis was resolved.

4 Observe and describe the mood changes in Americans during the Cuban Missile Crisis.

5 Describe your feelings about the new music in the 1950s called rock and roll.

6 Express your likes and dislikes about life in the 1950s.

7 Defend the *Brown v. Board of Education* decision.

8 Take a stance for or against America's entry into the Korean Conflict.

9 Take a stance for or against the Nuclear Arms Race.

10 Weigh alternatives to the Nuclear Arms Race toward global destruction.

11 Write an ethical code for testing nuclear weapons to protect mankind and the environment.

12 Write about the actions of Nikita Khrushchev during the Cuban Missile Crisis.

13 Write a personal poem about the Cold War.

14 List the priorities that America should have had toward civil rights in the 1950s.

15 Describe your feelings about America's quest to be the first nation to land a man on the moon.

16.1 Blackline Master • Interpersonal Activities

Living Through the Early Cold War Years

The Cuban Missile Crisis

The Soviet Union made a dangerous gamble in 1962 by placing over 40 nuclear missiles on the island of Cuba. Soviet leader Nikita Khrushchev made this bold and daring move that nearly caused a nuclear war.

President Fidel Castro of Cuba and Nikita Khruschev, both Communist and enemies of the United States, nearly caused a major confrontation between the superpowers. By placing missiles so close to the United States, the Soviets could launch a major offensive against America. The United States found the missiles through intelligence flights over Cuba. The Soviets first denied any missiles were in Cuba, then later stated that the missiles were defensive missiles. After several weeks of a scary scenario, the Soviets backed down and withdrew the missiles.

The world was saved from a nuclear war. In fact, this was the closest the two superpowers ever came to nuclear war.

Activity Options

1. Write a collaborative paper on the Cuban Missile Crisis.

2. Role-play President John Kennedy and Nikita Khrushchev during the Cuban Missile Crisis.

3. Reach a consensus explaining why the United States would not accept Soviet missiles in Cuba.

4. Debate the issue of America's refusal to lift the current trade embargo against Cuba.

Experience U.S. History! • Rickey Millwood
Kagan Publishing • 1 (800) 933-2667 • www.KaganOnline.com

16.2 Blackline Master • Musical/Rhythmic Activities

Living Through the Early Cold War Years

The '60s Rock

The 1960s saw a major change in music from the 1950s. Several new bands from other nations entered the United States and caused a musical frenzy that had never been experienced. The Beatles from England were the best known of all these groups. The Beatles were seen on the *Ed Sullivan Show*. Television, the new communication tool, exposed them to the entire nation.

The Beach Boys were another popular band in the 1960s. Based out of California, they rocked the nation with many songs about cars, girls, and exotic places. They were perhaps the biggest rival to any foreign band touring the nation.

During the mid 1960s, a popular song and dance called the twist swept the nation. This song was recorded by Chubby Checker. Millions called Twisters performed the dance as he sang.

The late 1960s produced many anti-Vietnam War songs. Singers such as Edwin Starr and "Country" Joe McDonald expressed their feelings toward the war through their music. These songs had such an impact that the Army would not allow soldiers to listen to them while in Vietnam. In 1969 a major rock festival took place in Woodstock, New York. Several hundred thousand young people attended this concert. This concert was probably the highlight of the hippie movement.

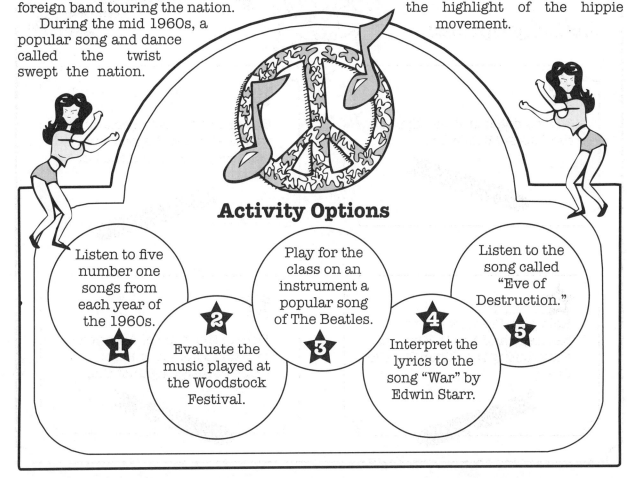

Activity Options

1. Listen to five number one songs from each year of the 1960s.
2. Evaluate the music played at the Woodstock Festival.
3. Play for the class on an instrument a popular song of The Beatles.
4. Interpret the lyrics to the song "War" by Edwin Starr.
5. Listen to the song called "Eve of Destruction."

Experience U.S. History! • Rickey Millwood
Kagan Publishing • 1 (800) 933-2667 • www.KaganOnline.com

16.3 Blackline Master • Bodily/Kinesthetic Activities

Living Through the Early Cold War Years

Walking on the Moon

The Soviet Union had given the United States quite a scare with its launching of the Sputnik—the first satellite launched into space. This event was followed by the Soviet Union placing a man in space before the United States.

America began to emphasize more math and science in schools to catch up with the Soviets. A race to the moon was on. President Kennedy stated that the United States would put a man on the moon by the end of the decade. That goal was accomplished in July 1969.

Americans held their breath as the lunar spacecraft touched down on the moon. The words "the eagle has landed" were heard. Millions of Americans watched as Neil Armstrong made the first moon walk. America had won a victory in propaganda during the Cold War; the United States had caught and surpassed the Soviets in the space race. Later, the United States would build space shuttles and space stations.

Activity Options

1. Perform a skit about America's landing on the moon.

2. Act out the role of Neil Armstrong as he took the first steps on the moon.

3. Visit the NASA Space Center in Florida or nasa.gov.

4. Visit the Air and Space Museum in Washington DC or nasm.si.edu.

5. Do a team presentation on the advancement of America's space program from 1964 to 1969.

Experience U.S. History! • Rickey Millwood
Kagan Publishing • 1 (800) 933-2667 • www.KaganOnline.com

16.4 Blackline Master • Visual/Spatial Activity

Living Through the Early Cold War Years

The Berlin Wall

Rifles sputtered and another person fell to the ground, desperately attempting to escape over the Berlin Wall. Attempting to escape from the Communist country of East Berlin was extremely dangerous and could easily result in death. No other symbol during the Cold War was hated more than the Berlin Wall.

Berlin had been a divided city since the end of World War II. Each day hundreds streamed out of East Germany and East Berlin to West Berlin in search of freedom. To Nikita Khruschev, the Soviet leader, this was embarrassing to the entire Communist world. He meant to stop this flow of traffic no matter the cost in dollars or lives. He decided to have the East German authorities build a wall of barbwire and concrete to seal off the border between East and West Berlin.

President Kennedy visited the wall and gave a speech condemning its construction. However, it remained a barrier between the free and Communist world until Soviet President Mikhail Gorbachev allowed it to be torn down in 1989.

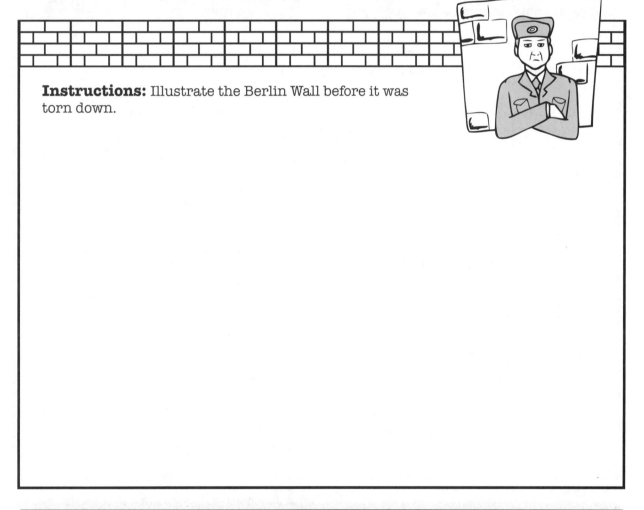

Instructions: Illustrate the Berlin Wall before it was torn down.

Chapter 17: The Time for Civil Rights (1954-1970)

The *Brown v. Board of Education* case in 1954 was one of the most important Supreme Court decisions in American history. It ended the Plessy decision of separate but equal. Unfortunately, many forms of segregation still existed in the nation. Way overdue, major Civil Rights legislation would come in 1964 and 1965. Led by Reverend Martin Luther King Jr., the Civil Rights Movement protested many injustices that African Americans had faced for years. It took federal legislation and authorities to enforce new laws aimed at ending all forms of segregation.

Verbal/Linguistic

1 Compare and contrast the Jim Crow laws with the former policy of apartheid in South Africa.

2 Discuss the impact of the *Brown v. Board of Education* Supreme Court decision in 1954.

3 Write a poem about African Americans in professional sports in the 1950s.

4 Write a biography about an important person during the Civil Rights Movement.

5 Write a newspaper article about Rosa Parks and the Montgomery Bus Boycott.

6 Compare the approach of Martin Luther King and Malcolm X to civil rights.

7 Read a primary document about the crisis at Little Rock Central High School.

8 Write a first-person account of a sit-in.

9 Read and analyze the 1964 Civil Rights Act.

10 Read Martin Luther King's I Have a Dream Speech.

11 Explain the major concepts in the 1965 Civil Rights Voting Act.

Logical/Mathematical

1 Analyze voting patterns in the South before 1954.

2 Graph the changes in African American voting patterns due to Civil Rights legislation passed in 1965.

3 Sequence the major events of the Civil Rights Movement, beginning in 1954.

4 Graph the number of registered African American voters before 1965.

5 Discover trends of resistance in Southern states to Civil Rights legislation.

6 List and organize facts about the March on Washington in 1963.

7 Evaluate the ideas of Malcolm X.

8 Brainstorm ideas about the goals of the Black Panthers.

9 Discover any patterns in the race riots across America in the 1960s.

10 Compare and contrast the ideas of any two Civil Rights leaders.

11 Prioritize the greatest accomplishments of the Civil Rights Movement.

Experience U.S. History! • Rickey Millwood
Kagan Publishing • 1 (800) 933-2667 • www.KaganOnline.com

Visual/Spatial

1 Make a poster about major Civil Rights leaders from 1954 to 1970.

2 Examine photos that show the attack on the Freedom Riders in Anniston, Alabama.

3 Draw a historical scene from the Civil Rights Movement.

4 Pretend you were a marcher with Dr. Martin Luther King Jr. in Selma, Alabama. Write about a famous protest march Dr. King led.

5 Examine photographs or video of the major Civil Rights leaders leading protests.

6 Create a PowerPoint of the following Civil Rights leaders: Martin Luther King Jr., Malcolm X, Stokely Carmichael, Elijah Muhammed, and Bobby Seale.

7 Create a political cartoon about the impact of the 1965 Civil Rights Voting Act.

8 Examine a video of Dr. Martin Luther King's speeches.

9 Design a postage stamp honoring those that led the way for Civil Rights.

10 Make a PowerPoint about the life of Rosa Parks.

Musical/Rhythmic

1 Examine the song lyrics of "We Shall Overcome."

2 Evaluate the impact that Motown music had on the Civil Rights Movement.

3 Listen to and interpret the song, "Eve of Destruction."

4 Listen to the lyrics of the song "Lift Every Heart and Sing."

5 Listen to the Civil Rights music of Mahalia Jackson.

6 Listen to the Civil Rights songs of Joan Baez.

7 Interpret the lyrical meanings to the song "Dancing in the Streets."

8 Find any patterns in Civil Rights music.

9 Write a song about a single event during the Civil Rights Movement.

10 Play on instruments several popular songs during the Civil Rights Movement for the class.

11 Evaluate Berry Gordy's position at Motown Records on Civil Rights protest songs.

12 Find a common theme between Southern spirituals and Civil Rights songs.

Chapter 17 continued
The Time for Civil Rights
(1954–1970)

★ Bodily/Kinesthetic

1 Act out the role of Rosa Parks as she refused to give up her seat on a bus in Montgomery, Alabama.

2 Role-play Dr. Martin Luther King Jr. giving his I Have a Dream Speech.

3 Visit places where Civil Rights demonstrations took place.

4 Pantomime concepts from the Civil Rights Movement. Have classmates guess each concept.

5 Create a play about a Civil Rights leader.

6 Perform a skit about the 1965 Civil Rights Voting Act.

7 Role-play the Supreme Court justices in the *Brown v. Board of Education* decision.

8 Role-play a newscaster covering the Selma, Alabama, March.

9 Create some crafts that pay tribute to the Civil Rights Movement.

10 Role-play a journalist interviewing a Freedom Rider about the attacks in Alabama.

11 Act out the role of Justice Thurgood Marshall in a Supreme Court decision that dealt with segregation laws.

★ Naturalist

1 Visit the Washington Monument, where Dr. Martin Luther King Jr. gave his I Have a Dream Speech.

2 Visit Selma, Alabama, where a major Civil Rights march took place.

3 Visit Anniston, Alabama, and read about the Freedom Riders.

4 Record changes in the developmental stages of the Civil Rights Movement across the Southern states.

5 Visit Memphis, Tennessee, and conduct research about the assassination of Dr. Martin Luther King Jr.

6 Examine and interpret photographs that illustrate the poverty in the deep South due to the Jim Crow laws.

7 Observe photographs of a segregated South before 1954.

8 Examine photographs of race riots fires in Los Angeles in 1965. Share with a partner your feelings about the riot.

9 Visit a place in your community where a Civil Rights demonstration or event took place.

10 Categorize the signs that Civil Rights marchers carried.

Experience U.S. History! • Rickey Millwood
Kagan Publishing • 1 (800) 933-2667 • www.KaganOnline.com

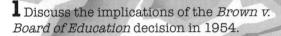

Interpersonal

1 Discuss the implications of the *Brown v. Board of Education* decision in 1954.

2 Reach a consensus on why the Southern states were so slow to react to the Brown decision.

3 Plan an event to honor a Civil Rights hero.

4 Share with others your thoughts on the Freedom Riders and dangers they encountered.

5 Research, and take turns giving reports on Supreme Court cases that eliminated different aspects of segregation from society.

6 Make a team project that traces the Civil Rights Movement from 1954 to 1970.

7 Do a team presentation on how music affected the Civil Rights movement.

8 Write a collaborative paper on any Civil Rights organization and its purpose.

9 Do a team presentation on the role of the NAACP during the 1960s.

10 Discuss with a partner the views Presidents Kennedy and Johnson had toward civil rights.

11 Conduct an interview with a participant from the Civil Rights Movement.

 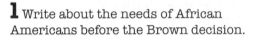

Intrapersonal

1 Write about the needs of African Americans before the Brown decision.

2 Defend in an essay the position Rosa Parks took on a bus in Montgomery.

3 Observe and discuss the mood changes in America during the Civil Rights Movement.

4 Think about the actions of Martin Luther King Jr. in Selma, Alabama. Then share your thoughts with a partner.

6 Write about the actions of Malcolm X in the Civil Rights Movement.

7 Take a stance to end all forms of segregation in America.

8 Write a personal poem about any individual that played a prominent role during the Civil Rights Movement.

9 Write about the actions that took place across America after the assassination of Dr. Martin Luther King Jr.

10 Describe your feelings about the Jim Crow laws, literacy tests, and poll taxes.

11 Form an action plan to register and encourage all U.S. citizens to participate in elections.

12 Reflect on the role that Dr. Martin Luther King Jr. played in American history. Write a letter to Dr. King expressing thanks for his contributions.

13 Defend the position by President Johnson to enforce the 1965 Civil Rights Voting Act.

14 Write about any Supreme Court decision that broke up some aspect of segregation in America.

15 Express your likes or dislikes toward the possibility of building a historical Civil Rights Museum in Washington DC.

Experience U.S. History! • Rickey Millwood
Kagan Publishing • 1 (800) 933-2667 • www.KaganOnline.com

The Time for Civil Rights

The Montgomery Bus Boycott

Imagine being told to give up your seat and move to the back of the bus because of your race. Such was the case in Montgomery, Alabama, in December 1955. Rosa Parks was seated on the fifth row when an incident occurred that had major repercussions.

The first four rows of the bus were reserved for whites. African Americans could be seated beginning with the fifth row, but the law stated that African Americans had to give up their seats and move to the back as additional whites entered the bus. Rosa was ordered to vacate her seat and move to the back of the bus as additional whites boarded. She refused to give up her seat and was arrested.

This event led to the Montgomery Bus Boycott. This movement was led by Dr. Martin Luther King Jr. Tempers flared and Dr. King's home was even bombed as the boycott continued for months. This event propelled Dr. King into the national spotlight as a leader for the Civil Rights Movement. Eventually, in November 1956, the United States Supreme Court ruled that buses could not be segregated.

Instructions: Write an essay to defend the actions of Rosa Parks as she refused to give up her seat on the fifth row of the bus.

17.2 Blackline Master • Interpersonal Activity

The Time for Civil Rights

The Freedom Riders

African Americans had been denied the right to vote in Southern states with the passage of the Jim Crow laws. They were restricted from voting by poll taxes and literacy tests. Brutal intimidation also kept them away from the polls. African Americans had tended to vote Republican because that was the party of Lincoln. However, African Americans suffered terribly during the Great Depression and began to switch parties and vote Democratic. Many people in the North wanted to see all Americans registered to vote and began a campaign through the South to register African Americans.

In 1961, Freedom Rides took place in the South. These rides tested the Supreme Court ruling to eliminate segregation at bus terminals. These riders were a mixture of different people willing to test the new laws. Brave Freedom Riders boarded a bus in Washington DC and headed for New Orleans. Some Southerners resented this campaign and violently attacked the Freedom Riders. At Anniston, Alabama, a Freedom Rider bus was bombed and the riders beaten as they got off the burning bus. Another group of riders was also beaten in Birmingham at a bus station.

President Kennedy could not depend on Southern legislators to protect these riders so he sent 500 marshals to the South. This event in 1961 demonstrated seven years after the Brown case that segregation was still very much alive in the Deep South. Major Civil Rights legislation would not come until 1964.

Instructions: In pairs, plan an event on May 14, to honor the Freedom Riders.

Experience U.S. History! • Rickey Millwood

17.3 Blackline Master • Verbal/Linguistic Activity

The Time for Civil Rights

The March on Washington

We have seen in our nation's history, several major marches on Washington DC. Coxey's March and the Bonus Army March both involved employment and money. In August 1963, a different kind of march took place. This was a march led by Dr. Martin Luther King Jr. for Civil Rights for all U.S. citizens. There, Dr. King gave his famous I Have a Dream Speech—one of the most touching and brilliant speeches made in American history. Dr. King delivered this speech in his elegant style. He traced American history in his speech from Emancipation to the current crisis in the nation over Civil Rights. In his speech, he stated what his vision would be for all Americans. His speech challenged Americans to recognize people for their intent and not the color of their skin.

In 1964 major Civil Rights legislation would be enacted. This legislation was aimed at employment and segregation in public facilities. In 1965, Civil Rights legislation was aimed primarily at voting. Dr. King's speech and the March on Washington led the way for major changes that were long overdue.

Instructions: Read Martin Luther King's I Have a Dream Speech. Write a summary of Dr. King's dream.

Experience U.S. History! • Rickey Millwood
Kagan Publishing • 1 (800) 933-2667 • www.KaganOnline.com

The Time for Civil Rights

Civil Rights Songs

Music has always played a part in major events in American history. The Civil Rights Movement was no exception. Imagine being in Washington DC in 1963 and hearing the songs that led the way for Civil Rights.

The most famous of all Civil Rights songs was "We Shall Overcome." Other popular songs included "Lift Ev'ry Heart and Sing", "In the Ghetto", and "Abraham, Martin, and John." Singers included African Americans and whites that wanted to see America free of racial injustice.

The great Civil Rights March on Washington DC in 1963 drew a crowd of 250,000. There in our nation's capital, many Civil Rights songs were performed by popular artists that joined the movement. Americans often express their feelings through songs; the Civil Rights Movement demonstrates that by an outpouring of music.

Instructions: Write your own song about one event during the Civil Rights Movement.

_____

_____

_____

_____

_____

_____

_____

_____

_____

_____

Chapter 18: The Era Of Vietnam (1954-1975)

Except for the Civil War, no other event has divided the nation more than the Vietnam Conflict of the 1960s and 1970s. American involvement in Southeast Asia was aimed at containing Communism. However, the conflict resulted in splitting the nation as the causalities mounted. Two years after America withdrew from Vietnam, Saigon fell to the Communists from the North. This experience left a bitter taste in the mouths of Americans for decades. Those who served in Vietnam did not receive the recognition that they so much deserved until the 1980s.

Verbal/Linguistic

1 Explain how America became involved in the Vietnam Conflict.

2 Complete a creative writing exercise on the Gulf of Tonkin Incident.

3 Interview a veteran that served in Vietnam and write a report on the interview.

4 Discuss the role that women played in the Vietnam Conflict.

5 Read about tactics of the Viet Cong.

6 Discuss how the 1968 election was affected by the conflict in Vietnam.

7 Write a paper describing the impact of the Tet Offensive.

8 Write a persuasive paper supporting or condemning America's involvement in Vietnam.

9 Write about the treatment of American POWs in Vietnam.

10 Discuss the impact the draft had on America's perception of the Vietnam Conflict.

11 Write a newspaper article about the decision to abandon Vietnam in 1973.

Logical/Mathematical

1 Create a time line for American involvement in Vietnam.

2 Graph the number of Americans sent to Vietnam each year from 1961 to 1973.

3 Analyze data that shows the financial cost of staying in Vietnam each year.

4 Calculate the amount of Agent Orange sprayed across Vietnam.

5 Create a chart that shows the number of deaths America suffered in Vietnam from 1961 until 1973.

6 Estimate the tonnage of bombs the United States dropped on Vietnam.

7 Graph the election results of the 1968 presidential election.

8 Organize facts about the Viet Cong.

9 Sequence the major events of the Vietnam Conflict.

Experience U.S. History! • Rickey Millwood
Kagan Publishing • 1 (800) 933-2667 • www.KaganOnline.com

Visual/Spatial

1 Watch the film *The Green Berets*.

2 Examine photographs of the topography of Vietnam after being sprayed with Agent Orange.

3 Design a poster about the effects of Agent Orange.

4 Create a PowerPoint of the major characters involved in the Vietnam Conflict.

5 Design a postage stamp honoring those who served in Vietnam.

6 Examine pictures of Vietnam protestors.

7 Locate and comment on a picture of a dramatic moment in the Vietnam Conflict.

8 Create a map that illustrates the Ho Chi Minh Trails.

9 Examine pictures of booby traps and tunnels in Vietnam.

10 Watch the film *No Time for Tears*.

11 Examine pictures of the Hanoi Hilton.

12 Design a book cover about the Vietnam Conflict.

13 Create a political cartoon about America's involvement in Vietnam.

14 Watch the television series *Vietnam the Television War*.

Musical/Rhythmic

1 Listen to 10 songs about the Vietnam Conflict.

2 Evaluate the impact that antiwar songs had upon the nation during the Vietnam Conflict.

3 Interpret the meaning to the lyrics "Ballad of the Green Beret."

4 Identify musicians that performed at the Woodstock Festival.

5 Interpret the lyrics to the song, "War," by Edwin Starr.

6 Play a song on an instrument about the Vietnam Conflict for the class.

7 Identify five groups or individuals that wrote or sang songs about the Vietnam Conflict.

8 Discuss how the Army attempted to prevent soldiers in Vietnam from listening to antiwar music.

9 Write a rap song about the Vietnam Conflict.

10 Listen to the song, "Ball of Confusion," by the Temptations.

11 Listen to the song, "Eve of Destruction," by Barry McGuire.

Chapter 18 continued
The Era Of Vietnam
(1954–1975)

Bodily/Kinesthetic

1 Act out the role of a young man drafted into the Army in 1968.

2 Act out the role of a Vietnam Conflict supporter.

3 Act out the role of a Vietnam Conflict protestor.

4 Conduct an interview of a soldier that was sprayed with Agent Orange.

5 Perform a skit about a veteran claiming Agent Orange gave him or her cancer.

6 Perform a dance that was popular during the Vietnam Conflict.

7 Role-play American POWs stating how they were treated in the Hanoi Hilton.

8 Role-play the presidential candidates in the 1968 election.

9 Design a monument honoring those who gave their lives in Vietnam.

10 Act out the role of a woman who served in Vietnam.

Naturalist

1 Visit the Vietnam Memorial Wall in Washington DC.

2 Attend a Veterans Day program honoring soldiers from past wars.

3 Examine pictures that show the natural vegetation of Vietnam.

4 Identify the major foods produced in Vietnam.

5 Label on the map the rivers in Vietnam.

6 Examine and comment on pictures of areas sprayed with Agent Orange in Vietnam.

7 Create a chart that demonstrates the average rainfall per month in Vietnam.

8 Graph temperature patterns in Vietnam.

9 Locate and discuss a picture showing the tunnels where the Viet Cong hid.

10 Find a picture of American soldiers going through rice paddies. Write a journal entry describing the experience as if you were a soldier.

11 Notice the flowers worn by hippies and flower children. Classify several of these flowers.

Experience U.S. History! • Rickey Millwood
Kagan Publishing • 1 (800) 933-2667 • www.KaganOnline.com

Interpersonal

1 Discuss as a class the major problems America confronted in Vietnam.

2 Reach a consensus to determine if America should have been involved in Vietnam for 12 years.

3 Practice criticizing the use of Napalm and Agent Orange in Vietnam.

4 Interview each other about the lottery draft.

5 Take turns stating why the Vietnam Conflict went so poorly for America.

6 Debate the policy of Containment and the Domino Theory.

7 Share with others your thoughts of the American strategies employed in Vietnam.

8 Make a team project to present patriotic and antiwar songs to the class.

9 Write papers as teams on the major events of the Vietnam Conflict.

10 Debate as a class the lessons America learned in Vietnam.

 ## Intrapersonal

1 Form an action plan that would have won a clear American victory in Vietnam.

2 Describe your feelings in an essay about America's involvement in Vietnam.

3 Write an ethical code of conduct that should have been followed in the treatment of American POWs.

4 Describe your feelings about the antiwar movement and the hippies.

5 Write about the actions of William Calley and the My Lai Massacre.

6 Weigh alternatives to the draft.

7 Write about the needs of American soldiers in Vietnam.

8 Defend the American position to defend South Vietnam from North Vietnam.

9 Write about how the Tet Offensive turned Americans against the war.

10 Express your likes and dislikes about America's involvement in Vietnam.

11 Defend a position by Richard Nixon to sign the Paris Accords and leave Vietnam in 1973.

12 Observe and discuss the mood changes in young Americans as the Vietnam Conflict lingered.

The Era Of Vietnam

Vietnam—The Decision to Stay or Leave

The United States had never lost a war and leaving Vietnam in 1973 was a difficult decision. Leaving without a clear-cut victory disturbed many Americans and still haunts the nation. Our country had spent billions of dollars in Vietnam and lost thousands of lives. The United States also abandoned South Vietnam, which fell to Communist North Vietnam in 1975.

Richard Nixon did not want to go down in history as the first U.S. president to lose a war. He unleashed a massive bombing attack on Vietnam, known as Operation Linebacker, and was finally able to negotiate a truce that got the United States out of Vietnam. This was the first conflict in U.S. history that America did not win.

Instructions: Write an essay that compares and contrasts our nation's involvement in Vietnam and Iraq.

The Era Of Vietnam

Agent Orange

In 1965, the United States began to spray a substance across Vietnam called Agent Orange, a highly controversial chemical. Over 20 million gallons were sprayed until 1970 during Operation Ranch Hand. The purpose of spraying this chemical was to eradicate the jungle growth in Vietnam and deny the Viet Cong a hiding place. Using this effective chemical, entire sanctuaries of hiding places were eliminated. Even now, large sections of Vietnam are still barren and contaminated.

After returning home from Vietnam, some veterans claimed that Agent Orange gave them cancer. The Army had not told the soldiers of the potential effects. Soldiers were never given any protective gear to march through jungles covered with this defoliant. Years later, some veterans received small compensation checks after lengthy hearings and decisions.

Today, scientific studies are being conducted in Vietnam to determine the long-term effects of Agent Orange on the environment, animals, and humans. There's no better place to study the chemical than where it was heavily sprayed for five years.

Activity Options

1. Debate the decision to spray Agent Orange across Vietnam in areas where American soldiers were present.

2. Do a team presentation on the immediate effects of spraying Agent Orange.

3. Reach a consensus on the importance of conducting studies on Agent Orange in Vietnam.

4. Discuss with a partner the possibility that Agent Orange causes birth defects.

5. Take turns condemning or supporting the U.S. army for using Agent Orange in Vietnam.

18.3 Blackline Master • Bodily/Kinesthetic Activities

The Era Of Vietnam

U.S. Military Women in Vietnam

Nearly three million Americans were sent to the jungles of Vietnam. Today, each survivor has his or her own unique story to tell about this episode in American history.

Women played a major role in Vietnam as they served primarily in the medical field. They desperately tried to save the lives of wounded American men. They witnessed ghastly scenes daily but had the strength and composure to perform their duties.

These brave, patriotic women served the nation in very difficult circumstances. Many times they were overwhelmed with the number of incoming wounded and had to make difficult decisions about which soldiers to attempt to save. It has been more than 30 years since the Vietnam Conflict ended, yet—many woman will never forget their chilling experience in Vietnam. These women who served and died—are now recognized at the Vietnam Women's Memorial in Washington DC.

Activity Options

1. Conduct an interview with any woman who served in Vietnam.

2. Act out the role of a nurse that served in Vietnam and allow the class to conduct an interview.

3. Perform a skit about a young lady in 1966 who is about to graduate from high school as she tries to convince her parents why she has decided to join the Army.

4. Perform any song performed by female entertainers that relates to the Vietnam Conflict.

5. Discuss with any woman between the ages of 54 and 65, her thoughts and memories about Vietnam.

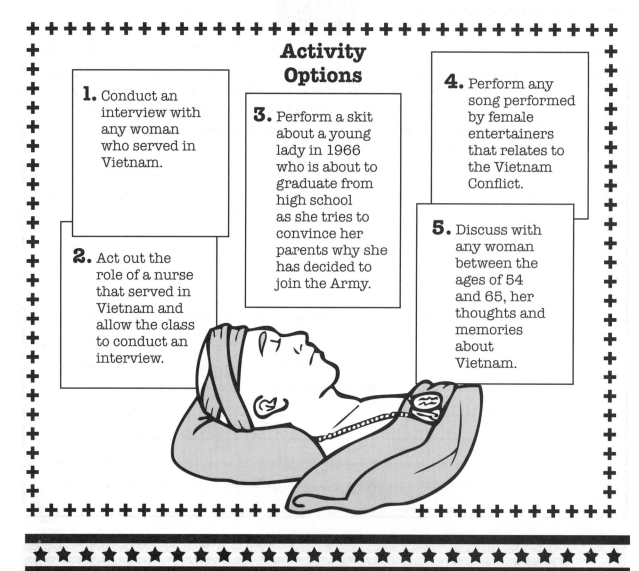

Experience U.S. History! • Rickey Millwood
Kagan Publishing • 1 (800) 933-2667 • www.KaganOnline.com

18.4 Blackline Master • Intrapersonal Activity

The Era Of Vietnam

The Kent State Massacre

Imagine attending college during the days of the Vietnam Conflict. The Tet Offensive in 1968 had turned the nation against the war. Demonstrations against the war were taking place nationwide and one became deadly at a college in Ohio.

In May 1970, a tragic event occurred on the campus of Kent State University. Students were protesting the Vietnam Conflict and some politicians thought the demonstrations were out of control.

The National Guard was sent out to suppress the demonstrations. To break up the crowd, guardsmen fired into the crowd of students. The shots killed four students and wounded nine others.

Rather than dying from bullets in Vietnam, young students died on the campus of their own college. This incident marked another sad, shocking episode in the Vietnam Conflict.

Instructions: Imagine you were a student at Kent State University and witnessed this event. Write a letter to your family back home and describe exactly what happened.

Chapter 19: Détente and Life Through the '70s
(1968-1980)

The 1970s saw a relief in tension between the superpowers. The term *détente* was used to define the new relationship between the United States and the Soviet Union. The two nations began to cooperate and trade. President Nixon made a historical visit to both the Soviet Union and to the People's Republic of China. The 1970s also showed Americans just how dependent they were on supplies of foreign petroleum.

Verbal/Linguistic

1 Explain the concept of "détente."

2 Write a newspaper article about the Strategic Arms Limitations Talks (SALT) agreement.

3 Discuss the implications of President Nixon's trip to China.

4 Write a persuasive paper urging cooperation between the United States and China.

5 Write a poem about Ping Pong Diplomacy.

6 Compare and contrast Nixon's visits to China and the Soviet Union.

7 Read *All the President's Men*.

8 Research how the Watergate Scandal brought down President Nixon.

9 Create slogans about the Ford and Carter administrations.

10 Perform a creative writing exercise about the Iranian Hostage Crisis in 1979.

11 Debate the decision by President Carter to boycott the 1980 Olympic Games in Moscow.

12 Discuss the implications of the Soviet invasion of Afghanistan.

Logical/Mathematical

1 List the causes and effects of President Nixon's visits to China and the Soviet Union.

2 Identify general principles in Nixon's foreign policy.

3 List or organize facts about the 1972 presidential election.

4 Sequence the events of the Watergate Scandal.

5 Make associations between the Watergate Scandal and political scandal in American history.

7 Debate whether President Ford should or should not have pardoned President Nixon.

9 Compare President Carter and President Wilson.

11 Contrast America's reaction to the Iranian Hostage Crisis and 9-11.

12 Examine and explain the rate of inflation during the Carter administration.

13 Graph the rate of employment in America from 1976 to 1980.

14 Evaluate President Carter's idea of returning the Panama Canal back to Panama.

Visual/Spatial

1 Examine political cartoons about the Watergate Scandal.

2 Watch video of President Nixon's resignation from the presidency.

3 Imagine you were President Nixon leaving the White House due to the Watergate Affair. Write about your feelings.

4 Make a poster about the issues in the 1976 election.

5 View video of the Iranian Hostage Crisis of 1979.

6 View photographs of Ayatollah Khomeini.

7 View the film *Not Without My Daughter*.

8 Create a PowerPoint about the presidency of Jimmy Carter.

9 Examine pictures of refugees escaping Southeast Asia in the 1970s.

10 Create a collage of photos representing the Iranian Hostage Crisis or the Soviet invasion of Afghanistan.

Musical/Rhythmic

1 Listen to Helen Reddy's song "I Am Woman."

2 Listen to the music of the Bee Gees.

3 Listen to disco songs performed by Donna Summer.

4 Evaluate the music of the 1970s.

5 Write a song about a political event of the 1970s.

6 Learn about the top 10 songs of the 1970s.

7 Compare and contrast the music of the 1960s with the 1970s.

8 Identify any popular musicals of the 1970s.

9 Listen to Vietnam War protest songs.

10 Determine how musical instruments changed during the 1970s.

11 Listen to the music of five famous bands from the 1970s.

Chapter 19 continued
Détente and Life Through the '70s
(1968–1980)

Bodily/Kinesthetic

1 Act out the role of Richard Nixon on his historical visit to China.

2 Act out the concept of Ping Pong Diplomacy.

3 Perform a skit about the gas shortage and gas lines in 1974.

4 Build a model of the Watergate Hotel.

5 Visit the Nixon Library in Yorba Linda, California.

6 Role-play the Watergate hearings and proceedings.

7 Act out the role of a person who learns his or her family member is being held hostage in Iran by Ayatollah Khomeini.

8 Role-play an athlete denied the opportunity to participate in the 1980 Olympics.

9 Perform a dance from the disco era.

10 Role-play a nuclear war protestor.

11 Role-play Jimmy Carter, Anwar Sadat, and Menachem Begin at the Camp David talks.

12 Role-play voters discussing the issues in the 1980 election.

Naturalist

1 Discuss how nuclear tests in the 1970s have effected the Earth.

2 Determine and discuss how Americans changed sources of energy in the early 1970s.

3 Discuss how the oil shortage in 1974 affected live in America.

4 Discuss the building of the Alaskan pipeline.

5 Determine and write about how wildlife was affected by the Alaskan Pipeline.

6 Graph the rising cost of oil from 1970 to 1976.

7 Record the function of the Environmental Protection Agency (EPA).

8 Record any changes in America's energy conservation after the 1974 oil embargo by the Organization of Petroleum Exporting Countries (OPEC).

9 Read and discuss the Endangered Species Act.

10 Discover any trends in control of automobile emission systems in the 1970s.

11 Create a log of changes that regulated the transporting or disposing of nuclear waste.

12 Record changes in laws to protect the oceans from toxic dumping.

Experience U.S. History! • Rickey Millwood
Kagan Publishing • 1 (800) 933-2667 • www.KaganOnline.com

Interpersonal

1 Discuss with a partner the court case *Roe v. Wade*.

2 Make a team project about the Fall of Saigon.

3 Share with others thoughts about the Watergate Affair.

4 Write a collaborative paper on President Nixon's foreign policy.

5 Solve the problems America faced as a result of an oil embargo in 1974.

6 Debate the pardon granted by President Ford to President Nixon.

7 Debate the decision by President Carter to allow Shah Pahlavi to escape from Iran and come to America.

8 Discuss the actions by President Carter at Camp David to bring Israel and Egypt together.

9 Do a team presentation on the 1980 Olympics Boycott.

10 Interview each other about the 1980 election issues.

11 In teams of four, write a summary of major Supreme Court decisions in the 1970s.

Intrapersonal

1 Describe your feelings about the *Roe v. Wade* decision.

2 Express your likes and dislikes about President Nixon.

3 Take a stance for Nixon's policy of détente toward the Soviet Union.

4 Defend the position by Richard Nixon to visit China in 1972.

5 Write about the actions of President Nixon during the Watergate Scandal.

6 Take a stance for or against the grain deals to the Soviet Union in 1972.

7 Describe your feelings about the SALT deal.

8 Write about the economic actions and policies of Gerald Ford as president.

9 Express your likes and dislikes about Jimmy Carter as president.

10 Write about the actions of President Carter as he tried to rescue the hostages in Iran.

11 Write about the actions of President Carter after the Soviet Union invaded Afghanistan.

12 Take a stance for or against the 1980 Olympics Boycott.

13 Describe your feelings about the American economy in the late 1970s.

14 Observe and discuss mood changes in Americans at the end of Carter's administration.

19.1 Blackline Master • Naturalist Activities

Détente and Life Through the '70s

The 1974 Oil Embargo Crisis

The boost in gasoline prices in fall 2005 reminds older Americans about another gasoline crisis. Through the 1960s and early 1970s, Americans were used to very cheap gasoline and oil prices. Gasoline was sold for about 25 cents per gallon. That would change in 1974. OPEC cut off oil sales to the United States and we were caught completely by surprise by this trade embargo. Americans were about to experience a gasoline shortage like they could have never imagined.

In October 1973, Egypt and Syria attacked Israel. America defended Israel and the Arab nations retaliated with an oil embargo against the United States. In winter 1974, oil shipments to America ceased and shortages occurred all over the nation. Gasoline tripled in price and long gas lines formed. Factories closed and the American economy was devastated. Oil was used as an economic weapon against the nation, and we felt the crunch for being dependent on foreign oil.

Desperate measures were enacted by our nation. A national speed limit law of 55 miles per hour was passed and Americans were urged to carpool. Americans were counselled to conserve and to buy gasoline on specific days of the week. Gasoline stations were closed on Sundays. Many Americans turned to small foreign cars to conserve fuel. America even built an oil pipeline through Alaska, but this had virtually no effect until years later. The oil crisis by OPEC definitely made the United States reassess its policy toward oil-rich Arab states.

Activity Options

1. Determine how much oil the United States imported in 1974 and how much is imported today.

2. Identify the American states that produce most of our nation's oil.

3. Record the measures taken in 1974 to relieve the oil embargo.

4. Describe any natural materials used as a source of heat or fuel due to the energy crisis.

5. Chart the route of the Alaskan Pipeline.

6. Identify the nations that currently supply America with most of its oil.

7. Describe how the rise in gasoline prices during 2005 affected the lives of Americans.

19.2 Blackline Master • Interpersonal Activity

Détente and Life Through the '70s

The Watergate Scandal

American history has been marked by all types of scandals. Several presidents have had Congressional charges brought against them but escaped being removed from office. The Nixon administration was to be no exception from scandal. President Nixon had been elected twice however, in 1974 he was forced out of office over the Watergate Affair. There is little doubt that he would have been removed from the presidency by Congress.

The Watergate Scandal involved a break-in and a cover-up by the Nixon administration: tried to spy on the Democratic Party and gain an advantage in the 1972 presidential election. The burglars were apprehended and details of a cover-up were revealed. The president recorded all his conversations in the White House. He did this for historical purposes, but these tapes would now be used against him. He tried to claim that it was his executive privilege not to turn over the tapes, but the Supreme Court ruled against him.

The nation was shocked to see the President step down. He had said, "I'm not a crook." This was the first time in American history that a president stepped aside.

Several of Nixon's top officials went to prison, but Nixon did not. Vice President Ford became president and pardoned Nixon for all matters pertaining to Watergate. The decision to pardon Nixon perhaps cost President Ford the election in 1976 against Jimmy Carter.

Instructions: As a team, examine and report on the scandals listed below.

SCANDAL	TEAM
A. Whiskey Ring	
B. Crédit Mobilier	
C. Tea Pot Dome	
D. Iran Contra	
E. Clinton–Lewinsky	

19.3 Blackline Master • Intrapersonal Activity

Détente and Life Through the '70s

Sports and Games During the Cold War

Watching intense sporting events between the United States and the Soviet Union during the 1970s and 1980s aroused much national pride and honor. These nations were bitter rivals in the political and sporting arenas. The athletes were often pressured to defeat their opponent for political reasons. This was the case in the famous chess championship between Boris Spassky of the Soviet Union and Bobby Fischer of the United States. Fischer won that match and the world championship.

The Olympics, an event that brings harmony between nations, became a substitute for war between the superpowers. Which nation would win the most gold medals? Which athletes would hear their national anthem played? Which team sports would each nation dominate? These questions surfaced at the Olympics until the Cold War ended. Did the Ancient Greeks intend for the Olympics to be played this way? Were athletes being used as pawns for national glory?

Two dramatic moments unfolded during the 1970s. In 1972, the United States lost a controversial basketball game to the Soviet Union. This was the first time an American team had ever lost a basketball game in the Olympics. In 1976, The American all-star college hockey team defeated a much more experienced hockey team from the Soviet Union. American goalie Jim Craig was draped with the American flag over his shoulders. This victory in hockey inspired the movie, *Miracle on Ice*.

In 1980, the Olympics were held in Moscow, but the United States did not participate. President Jimmy Carter decided that the American team would boycott the Olympics due to the Soviet invasion of Afghanistan. In 1984, the Soviet Union did not participate in the Olympics in Los Angeles. The Olympics involved International politics during the Cold War.

Instructions: Imagine you were an American athlete preparing for the 1980 Olympics in Moscow and just learned the U.S. team would boycott the games. Describe how you feel.

_____
_____
_____
_____
_____
_____
_____

Experience U.S. History! • Rickey Millwood
Kagan Publishing • 1 (800) 933-2667 • www.KaganOnline.com

19.4 Blackline Master • Logical/Mathematical Activity

Détente and Life Through the '70s

The Iran Crisis

The Carter administration faced a sticky situation in fall 1979 as the American embassy in Tehran, Iran, was seized by forces that were extremely anti-American. American embassy employees would be threatened and held captive for 444 days. Would this event cost President Carter the 1980 election?

In February, 1979, Ayatollah Khomeini overthrew Shah Pahlavi in Iran. The shah had been friends with several American presidents, and America had supported him for decades. He kept oil coming to America; the United States supplied him with military weapons and protected him from Communism.

The shah fled Iran and came to the United States to escape the wrath of Ayatollah Khomeini. The shah was dying of cancer and was allowed to come to New York to receive treatment. The Ayatollah demanded the return of the shah so he could be executed. However, President Carter would not deport this long-time American friend. Thus the stage was set for hostility between Iran and the United States.

Radicals in Iran seized the American embassy and the American diplomats. They demanded the return of the shah and threatened to execute the Americans held captive.

President Carter attempted to negotiate for and rescue the hostages. Both plans failed miserably. Americans began to perceive the nation's pride at stake.

President Cater was trying to keep the hostages alive and negotiate for their release. The shah left the United States for Panama, but the hostages were still held. Finally, the shah returned to Egypt where he died. The hostages were still not released.

In 1980, President Reagan was elected and the hostages were released on Inauguration Day. Relations between the two nations have been strained since 1979. Today, the United States is concerned with the threat of weapons of mass destruction being produced in Iran.

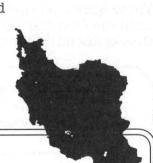

Instructions: List the events of the Iranian Hostage Crisis below. On a separate sheet of paper, sequence the events using a chain-graphic organizer.

Chain Graphic Organizer: Event 1 — Event 2 — Event 3 — Event 4

Experience U.S. History! • Rickey Millwood
Kagan Publishing • 1 (800) 933-2667 • www.KaganOnline.com

Chapter 20: The Conclusion of the Cold War and New Challenges (1990-2000)

The tearing down of the Berlin Wall and the breakup of the Soviet Union brought an end to the Cold War. Even though the Cold War concluded in the early 1990s, America would soon face new challenges in the Middle East. Saddam Hussein, President of Iraq, invaded Kuwait. America defended Kuwait through Operation Desert Storm. The 1990s were prosperous times through the Clinton administration. Many social and environmental issues made headline news through these years.

Verbal/Linguistic

1 Share ideas about Ronald Reagan's presidency and his determination to restore pride in Americans.

2 Complete a descriptive writing exercise about America's air strikes against Libya in 1986.

3 Read an article about the Iran-Contra Affair.

4 Write a research paper about the occupation of Kuwait by Iraq.

5 Create a word web about Operation Desert Storm.

6 Discuss President George Bush's role in ending the Cold War.

7 Discuss the collapse of the Berlin Wall.

8 Communicate ideas about the breakup of the Soviet Union.

9 Compare and contrast President Clinton's military policy with the policy of President Reagan.

10 Write a play about the 2000 presidential election returns in Florida.

Logical/Mathematical

1 Analyze data about the impact of the Reagan tax cuts.

2 Contrast the economic views of President Franklin Roosevelt and President Ronald Reagan.

3 Graph the rate of inflation from 1980 to 1988.

4 Sequence the events that led to the American air strike against Libya in 1986.

5 Sequence the events that led to Operation Desert Shield.

6 Synthesize ideas about Operation Desert Storm.

7 Compare and contrast Operation Desert Storm with Operation Iraqi Freedom.

8 Brainstorm ideas about the 1992 election.

9 Make predictions about America's economy after the end of the Cold War.

10 Discover trends in Supreme Court decisions through the 1990s.

11 Discover any trends in television programs or movies through the 1990s.

12 Analyze the election data from the 2000 presidential election.

Visual/Spatial

1 Create a postcard about an event during the Reagan administration.

2 Examine and interpret a political cartoon about the Iran-Contra affair.

3 Watch a video of Oliver North and the Iran-Contra hearings.

4 Sketch a picture of the tearing down of the Berlin Wall.

5 Examine a picture of President Reagan meeting with Mikhail Gorbachev.

6 Create a political cartoon of the military buildup under President Reagan.

7 Create a political cartoon of President Reagan's economic tax cuts.

8 Make a crossword puzzle about Operation Desert Storm.

9 Design a postage stamp about a major political or social event from 1981 to 2002.

10 Watch a video of the opening ceremony of the 1996 Olympic Games.

11 Create a PowerPoint about the collapse of Communism in Eastern Europe.

12 Create a PowerPoint of the major events of the 1990s.

13 Create a political cartoon about President Clinton's impeachment.

14 Draw a scene in Florida about the 2000 presidential election.

Musical/Rhythmic

1 Evaluate music from the 1980s.

2 Listen to the song, "In America," by Charlie Daniels.

3 Listen to the song, "God Bless the USA," by Lee Greenwood.

4 Learn about the major changes in musical instruments in the 1980s.

5 Listen to the music of Garth Brooks.

6 Interpret the lyrics of a song related to a social event in the 1980s.

7 Write a report on the impact of music videos.

8 Write about the changes in musical technology through the 1990s.

9 Listen to the song "We Are the World."

10 Listen to any song associated with AIDS research.

11 Trace the history of rap music.

12 Create a PowerPoint of rap music groups through the 1990s.

13 Create a rap song about the 2000 presidential election.

14 Perform a popular dance from either the 1980s or 1990s.

Experience U.S. History! • Rickey Millwood
Kagan Publishing • 1 (800) 933-2667 • www.KaganOnline.com

Chapter 20 continued

The Conclusion of the Cold War and New Challenges (1990–2000)

⭐ Bodily/Kinesthetic

1 Perform a skit about the nuclear accident at Three Mile Island.

2 Role-play a scientist speaking about a nuclear winter.

3 Examine a piece of the Berlin Wall.

4 Act out the role of a baseball fan at the 1989 World Series in San Francisco when an earthquake occurred.

5 Role-play a newscaster at the Kennedy Space Center when the Challenger accident took place.

6 Act out the role of Colin Powell after the Iraqi invasion of Kuwait.

7 Perform a skit about Desert Storm.

8 Role-play George Bush, Ross Perot, and Bill Clinton in the 1992 presidential election.

9 Role-play a reporter covering the Oklahoma City Bombing.

10 Act out the role of a concerned voter in Florida during the recount of the 2000 presidential election.

⭐ Naturalist

1 Examine photographs of the Mount St. Helens eruption in 1980.

2 Research the cause of the nuclear accident at Three Mile Island.

3 Research the Chernobyl accident in the Soviet Union.

4 Research the spotted owl controversy through the 1990s.

5 View photographs or video of the space shuttle Challenger covered with ice just before it was launched in 1986. Use these photographs to protest the decision made to launch the Challenger.

6 Observe the changes in Yellowstone Park due to a major fire in 1987.

7 Record changes in Alaska due to the Exxon Valdez accident.

8 Compare and contrast the 1906 San Francisco Earthquake with the 1989 San Francisco Earthquake.

9 Examine photos of the terrain American soldiers faced in Operation Desert Storm. Describe the photos to a partner.

10 Record any changes in pollution laws forbidding cruise ships from dumping waste into the oceans.

11 Examine photos of fires in Kuwait set by Iraqi soldiers during Operation Desert Storm.

12 Classify theories and predictions about a nuclear winter.

Experience U.S. History! • Rickey Millwood
Kagan Publishing • 1 (800) 933-2667 • www.KaganOnline.com

Interpersonal

1 Discuss with a partner the appointment of Sandra Day O'Connor as a Supreme Court justice.

2 Discuss with a partner the decision to launch the space shuttle Challenger even though it was covered with ice.

3 Do a team presentation on the fall of Communism in Eastern Europe.

4 Reach a consensus explaining why the Soviet Union collapsed.

5 Solve as a team the challenge to account for all of the former Soviet Union's nuclear materials.

6 Do a team presentation on the Iran-Contra affair.

7 Do a team presentation on the implications of the Iraqi invasion of Kuwait.

8 Share with others America's strategy to quickly win Operation Desert Storm.

9 Interview each other about Geraldine Ferraro's role in the 1984 presidential election.

10 Write a collaborative paper on President Clinton's impeachment process.

11 Discuss the impact that the Internet has on America.

12 Do a team presentation of the history of AIDS in America.

Intrapersonal

1 Prioritize items on President Reagan's agenda in his first term.

2 Describe your feelings about Sandra Day O'Connor's appointment to the Supreme Court.

3 Observe and discuss mood changes in Americans after a number of Savings and Loan institutions closed.

4 Defend the actions of President George Bush in Operations Desert Shield and Desert Storm.

5 Write about the actions of Ross Perot in the 1992 presidential election.

6 Express your likes and dislikes about the terrorist policy of President Clinton.

7 Write about any new medical breakthroughs in the 1990s.

8 Weigh alternatives to relying on OPEC nations for our gasoline.

9 Meditate on the major domestic issues of the 1990s. Create a log of your thoughts.

10 Observe mood changes in Los Angeles after the Rodney King verdict.

11 Describe your feelings about the O.J. Simpson trial.

12 Defend or criticize National American Free Trade Agreement (NAFTA).

13 Take a stance to continue space research despite recent space accidents.

Experience U.S. History! • Rickey Millwood
Kagan Publishing • 1 (800) 933-2667 • www.KaganOnline.com

20.1 Blackline Master • Verbal/Linguistic Activity

The Conclusion of the Cold War and New Challenges

Reagan Kept America Safe

President Reagan believed America could be safer during the Cold War if a defensive missile system was placed above the United States—much like an umbrella. He began a program called Strategic Defensive Initiative. It was commonly known as Star Wars. The purpose of this plan was to knock out incoming ballistic missiles with a system of satellites that could shoot laser beams at the missiles. This project has not been completed.

Another way to keep America safe was to immediately respond if attacked by terrorists. In 1986, Libyan terrorists bombed a nightclub in Berlin, Germany, killing a large number of people. This was a club where American soldiers often gathered. Evidence pointed directly to Libyan President Muammar Qaddafi. President Reagan had a tough policy toward terrorists and immediately went after the person most responsible for the attack. President Reagan ordered five American aircraft to attack Libya and eliminate Muammar Qaddafi. The raid destroyed Qaddafi's home and killed his daughter, but the Libyan leader escaped. The raid killed 40 Libyans and demonstrated that President Reagan would deal swiftly with terrorists.

Instructions: Create a mind map of the Cold War.

Experience U.S. History! • Rickey Millwood
Kagan Publishing • 1 (800) 933-2667 • www.KaganOnline.com

The Conclusion of the Cold War and New Challenges

Ecological Disaster in Alaska

Imagine seeing millions of gallons of thick black crude washing in the pristine Alaskan water. Such was the sight in March of 1989. The Exxon Valdez oil tanker hit a reef, causing the worst ecological disaster in U.S. history. Up to 30 million gallons of oil spilled into Prince William Sound. Thousands of birds, otters, and fish perished.

Captain Joseph Hazelwood was held accountable for the Valdez accident. He was charged with being drunk at the time of the accident, but that charge was removed at his trial.

The accident cost Exxon several billion dollars for cleanup and in fines. The long-term effects of this accident are still being studied. Man's dependency on oil comes with a high price tag of ecological risks.

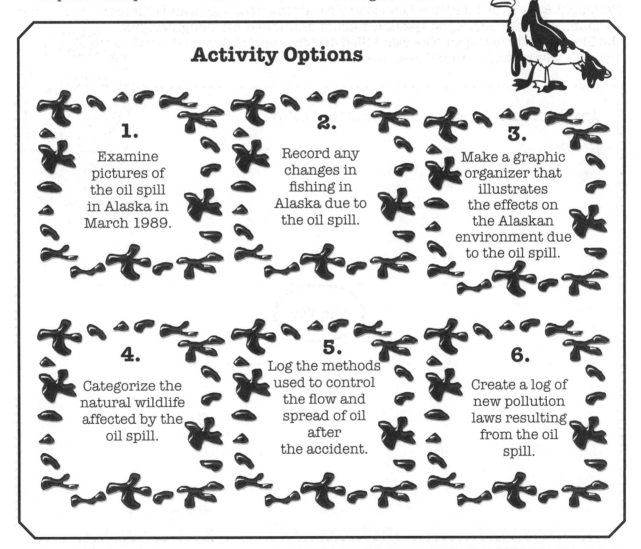

Activity Options

1. Examine pictures of the oil spill in Alaska in March 1989.

2. Record any changes in fishing in Alaska due to the oil spill.

3. Make a graphic organizer that illustrates the effects on the Alaskan environment due to the oil spill.

4. Categorize the natural wildlife affected by the oil spill.

5. Log the methods used to control the flow and spread of oil after the accident.

6. Create a log of new pollution laws resulting from the oil spill.

20.3 Blackline Master • Logical/Mathematical Activity

The Conclusion of the Cold War and New Challenges

Operation Desert Shield

In August 1990, Iraq invaded the nation of Kuwait. Iraq was desperate for money due to a long war with its neighbor Iran. Saddam Hussein believed he could invade and conquer Kuwait in a short time. However, he gambled incorrectly that he could keep Kuwait as a part of Iraq. The world condemned the invasion and the United States took the lead in driving Iraq out of Kuwait.

President George Bush warned Saddam Hussein to withdraw from Kuwait, but he refused and totally ignored a resolution by the United Nations. The United States took immediate action and sent a large force to Saudi Arabia to prevent further Iraqi aggression. This was called Operation Desert Shield.

In winter 1991, President Bush decided to unleash the U.S. Air Force on Iraq. Iraq took a severe pounding for weeks, and then the United States invaded. Saddam then launched missiles at Israel in an attempt to break up the coalition against him, but this plan failed. In a matter of hours after the ground war started, Iraq was defeated. Iraq agreed to withdraw from Kuwait, and the United States left Saddam Hussein in power. Many Americans felt an opportunity to remove Saddam had slipped away.

Instructions: Create a time line of actions taken by the United Nations after the Iraqi invasion of Kuwait until the end of Desert Storm.

Experience U.S. History! • Rickey Millwood
Kagan Publishing • 1 (800) 933-2667 • www.KaganOnline.com

20.4 Blackline Master • Intrapersonal Activity

The Conclusion of the Cold War and New Challenges

America Wins the Cold War in 1991

In the late 1980s, the Cold War came to an abrupt end. President Reagan had urged Mr. Gorbachev of the Soviet Union to tear down the Berlin Wall. In 1989, it came down. German reunification soon followed. The Soviet Union also dissolved, and the nations of Eastern Europe broke free of Communism.

The economy of the Soviet Union was in shambles and simply could not continue to prop up dictators and keep up the Arms Race. The Russian invasion of Afghanistan had drained the nation. Mr. Gorbachev, the last president of the Soviet Union, refused to use military force. In a matter of weeks, all of Eastern Europe was free. The Warsaw Pact was dissolved and many Americans took a deep breath of relief. The Soviet Union was no more—it became independent states.

During the Cold War most Americans lived with the threat of an all-out nuclear war. Now many people saw that threat end and a chance for world peace. The United States had won the Cold War but would soon face other threats.

The end of the Cold war stimulated the economy of America. Government expenses were shifted from defense to domestic spending, and new markets were opened all across Eastern Europe. The 1990s were prosperous times for Americans.

Instructions: Take a stance to remove nuclear missiles to make the world a safer place. Write a personal report on your beliefs of nuclear missiles.

Chapter 21: Recent Events in Our Nation's History

(2001–2005)

September 11, 2001, will forever be remembered as one of the most tragic days in American history. President George W. Bush immediately took action to find the terrorists responsible for the dastardly act against the United States. President Bush ousted the Taliban in Afghanistan and removed the Iraqi dictator Saddam Hussein from power. Americans faced natural disasters in 2005 as a series of intense hurricanes slammed into the Southern states.

★ Verbal/Linguistic ★

1 Write a poem or a descriptive piece about the attack on America on 9-11.

2 Share ideas about the terrorist group Al-Qaeda.

5 Debate the decision to invade Afghanistan after the attack on 9-11.

6 Read about Osama bin Laden's past terrorist activities.

7 Compare and contrast Operations Iraqi Freedom and Desert Storm.

8 Debate the decision to invade Iraq by President George W. Bush.

9 Explain the concept of weapons of mass destruction.

11 Write a newspaper article about the capture of Saddam Hussein.

12 Write a persuasive paper to keep troops in, or withdraw troops from Iraq.

13 Discuss the actions of the Federal Emergency Management Agency (FEMA) after Hurricane Katrina slammed into Mississippi and Louisiana.

14 Write a persuasive paper about the need for stronger levees in New Orleans to withstand powerful hurricanes.

★ Logical/Mathematical ★

1 Calculate the cost of the war in Iraq in terms of dollars and lives and evaluate the cost-to-benefit ratio.

2 Sequence events of 9-11 on a time line.

3 Evaluate America's response to make our nation safer from terrorists.

4 Brainstorm ideas to protect our nation from future terrorist attacks.

5 Predict the result of America's invasion of Iraq.

6 Make predictions about the number of years America will be involved in Iraq.

7 Select any three hurricanes that hit the United States in 2004 or 2005 and determine the economic damage of these storms.

8 Graph and analyze the price of gasoline from 1996 to 2006.

9 Create a survey to determine how gas prices affect driving habits.

10 Compare and contrast the 1974 oil crisis in 1974 with the oil crisis in 2005.

11 List and organize facts about the 2004 presidential election.

Experience U.S. History! • **Rickey Millwood**
Kagan Publishing • 1 (800) 933-2667 • www.KaganOnline.com

Visual/Spatial

1 Build a model of the World Twin Trade Centers.

2 Chart the route of the planes that crashed into the Twin Towers and Pentagon.

3 Take photographs where the terrorist attacks took place in America on 9-11.

4 Watch a video showing the Twin Trade Towers slammed by jets.

5 Design a postage stamp honoring the heroes on 9-11.

6 Watch video of President Bush's reaction to the attacks on 9-11.

7 View video of President Bush stating America would retaliate against the attacker on 9-11.

8 View video of New York Mayor Rudy Giuliani organizing relief efforts after 9-11.

9 Create a PowerPoint about the events of 9-11.

10 Create a PowerPoint about the American soldiers sent to Afghanistan and Iraq.

11 Imagine and write about how 9-11 changed life forever in America.

12 Design a memorial for the fallen soldiers in Afghanistan and Iraq.

13 Examine video of the damage caused by recent hurricanes in Florida, Alabama, Mississippi, and Louisiana.

14 Draw a scene of devastation caused by Hurricane Katrina.

 Musical/Rhythmic

1 Listen to Alan Jackson's "Where Were You?"

2 Listen to Toby Keith's "The Angry American."

3 Compose a song about 9-11.

4 Interpret the lyrics to any song about 9-11.

5 Write a song about the capture of Saddam Hussein.

6 Compare and contrast the music of 2005 with the music of a century earlier.

7 Listen to four different types of music heard on the radio in 2005.

8 Write a song about an event during the administration of George W. Bush.

9 Listen to "Where the Stars and Stripes and Eagles Fly" by Aaron Tippin.

10 Perform a song for the class about an event between 2000–2005.

11 Discuss the impact that musical videos have upon teenagers.

12 Write a jingle about a new product that will be a success in the 21st century.

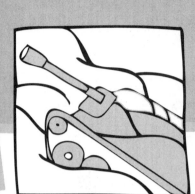

Chapter 21 continued
Recent Events in Our Nation's History (2001-2005)

Bodily/Kinesthetic

1 Act out the role of a Twin Trade Center survivor from the attack of 9-11.

2 Visit the places where the terrorist attacks on 9-11 took place.

3 Role-play a voter in the 2004 Presidential election.

4 Perform a skit about a soldier returning from Afghanistan or Iraq.

5 Perform a skit about the capture of Saddam Hussein.

6 Role-play Condoleezza Rice in supporting the president's decision to invade Iraq.

7 Role-play the administration in FEMA after Hurricane Katrina slammed into the Gulf Region in 2005.

8 Create a project on energy conservation after the rapid rise in price of gasoline.

9 Role-play a citizen complaining about the rapid rise of gasoline of over $3.50 per gallon in 2005.

10 Design a computer game about recent events in American history.

Naturalist

1 Visit the location of the former Twin Trade Towers.

2 Write a report about the building materials used in the Twin Trade Towers.

3 Observe through video the damage done by recent hurricanes in Florida and Mississippi.

4 List the characteristics of the levees in New Orleans.

5 Record the changes in New Orleans as result of Hurricane Katrina.

6 Examine damage done to oil rigs in the Gulf of Mexico as a result of hurricanes.

7 Classify by size and destruction three hurricanes of 2005.

8 Interview a soldier about the terrain and weather in Iraq or Afghanistan.

9 Determine the weather's affect on the 2004 presidential election.

10 Create a journal describing a major U.S. building or construction project taking place in the due to a hurricane.

Experience U.S. History! • **Rickey Millwood**
Kagan Publishing • 1 (800) 933-2667 • www.KaganOnline.com

★ Interpersonal

1 Debate how America was vulnerable to a terrorist attack on 9-11.

2 Share with others your thoughts about America's War on Terrorism.

3 Share with others your views on America's war in Iraq.

4 Discuss with classmates the reasons behind the war in Iraq.

5 Take turns stating America's greatest challenges in the 21st century.

6 Form solutions to five major problems America will confront in the next 10 years.

7 Do a team presentation on America's challenge to make our nation safe from terrorism.

8 Write a collaborative paper on the danger of weapons of mass destruction.

9 Interview each other about changes that could be made to the Social Security System.

10 Discuss the issue of the rising cost of prescription medicines in America.

11 Reach a consensus on the major issues the Supreme Court will face in the near future.

12 Discuss America's future role in the United Nations.

★ Intrapersonal

1 Defend or condemn the decision by President George W. Bush to invade Iraq.

2 Take a stance on the ethical treatment of prisoners of war from Iraq.

3 Choose between financing the war in Iraq or putting more money into hurricane relief. Explain your choice in writing.

4 Write about the needs of hurricane victims in Mississippi, Louisiana, and Florida.

5 Prioritize the needs of American soldiers stationed in Afghanistan and Iraq.

6 Express your likes and dislikes about the Homeland Security Act.

7 Weigh alternatives to sending the National Guard to Iraq.

8 Observe and discuss the mood changes in America after 9-11-01.

9 Write about the actions of President George W. Bush, immediately following 9-11.

10 Think about the actions of Congress as they investigate price gouging by major oil companies.

Experience U.S. History! • Rickey Millwood
Kagan Publishing • 1 (800) 933-2667 • www.KaganOnline.com

21.1 Blackline Master • Visual/Spatial Activity

Recent Events in our Nation's History

Attack On America: 9-11-01

On September 11, 2001, a major terrorist strike took place against the United States. The nation was totally unprepared for the events that unfolded. Four jets were high-jacked by Al-Qaeda terrorists. Two were flown into the World Trade Centers; one crashed into the Pentagon. Both of the Twin Towers collapsed, killing thousands. The fourth jet wrecked in a field in Pennsylvania as American passengers fought the terrorists for control of the plane.

Millions of Americans watched on television and were horrified by this event. Who had engineered such a plot against America? President George W. Bush responded by vowing to retaliate against the attackers. The chief plotter, Osama bin Laden, was operating his terrorist network out of Afghanistan.

America was stunned this day—just like the day Pearl Harbor was attacked. America would begin its strike against terrorism with an invasion of Afghanistan and the overthrow of the Taliban.

Instructions: Design a monument for the victims of 9-11.

Experience U.S. History! • Rickey Millwood
Kagan Publishing • 1 (800) 933-2667 • www.KaganOnline.com

21.2 Blackline Master • Intrapersonal Activity

Recent Events in our Nation's History

The Hunt for Osama bin Laden

Osama bin Laden, the world's most feared terrorist had masterminded the devastating 9-11 attack on the United States. President George W. Bush was furious over the attack and vowed to hunt down bin Laden.

American military intelligence felt certain that he was hiding in Afghanistan, a lawless nation under the command of the Taliban. The United States demanded that the Taliban turn bin Laden over, but they refused. The United States organized an attack on Afghanistan and overthrew the Taliban.

The United States tried to capture bin Laden, but he was able to escape— perhaps in the region of Tora Bora.

Since 9-11-01, the United States has placed a $25 million bounty on bin Laden. He is a ruthless killer the United States will never cease to hunt. With the end of the Cold War, Americans felt safer. However, terrorists who are willing to stop at nothing proved that all precautions must be taken to make our nation safe from future attacks.

Instructions: Write a personal poem about 9-11.

Recent Events in our Nation's History

Operation Iraqi Freedom

The United States began an attack on Iraq in 2003 in an attempt to overthrow Saddam Hussein. President George W. Bush was convinced that Saddam Hussein was making weapons of mass destruction to use against the United States. The president also believed that Iraq was being used as a base for Al-Qaeda.

Saddam had denied United Nations inspectors access into parts of Iraq to search for weapons. There was no doubt he had used chemical weapons before on the Kurds and on Iran. He had also invaded Kuwait and had planned to assassinate former President George H. Bush. It was further believed that he had assisted Osama bin Laden in the attack on 9-11-01.

The United States invaded and overthrew Saddam's regime. The Iraqi army was quickly routed and Saddam was later captured. His two sons were killed in a bloody battle.

No evidence was found of weapons of mass destruction, and this was a major issue in the 2004 presidential election. However, Americans were not willing to change presidents in the middle of this war with Iraq. President Bush was re-elected over John Kerry. There remains some speculation that the CIA gave the president incorrect information about weapons of mass destruction. President Bush contended that America was safer with Saddam Hussein out of the picture.

Wars are unpredictable. Iraq was no exception. Insurgents began to immediately attack Iraqis, joined American soldiers, and any Americans in Iraq. The price to fight terrorism is high in the cost of dollars and lives.

Activity Options

1. Debate the issue to invade Iraq in 2003, with a war already going on in Afghanistan.

2. Share with others the dangers American soldiers face in Iraq.

3. Take turns discussing the plan to suppress insurgents in Iraq.

4. Discuss with a partner the reasons why the United States invaded Iraq.

5. Role-play American soldiers returning from Iraq.

6. Share with other your thoughts on re-instating the draft in America.

21.4 Blackline Master • Naturalist Activities

Recent Events in our Nation's History

Natural Disasters

In 2004 and 2005, the United States was hit by a series of several potent category-four hurricanes. These storms contributed to deaths, caused billions of dollars in damage, and left thousands homeless. Florida and the Gulf Coast states were battered by these intense hurricanes. These storms have greatly affected the American economy.

In September 2005, Hurricane Katrina delivered a devastating blow to the nation. Massive damage was done to Mississippi, Florida, Alabama, and Louisiana. Americans were trapped in New Orleans as the levees broke. The city was instantly flooded. Tens of thousands were left homeless.

FEMA has been sharply criticized for an inadequate response. But, Americans all over the nation poured their hearts out to hurricane victims. Communities all over America set up shelters for homeless victims, and churches began to place victims in adequate housing.

We as a nation have overcome great challenges. This rugged determination, from the time of Jamestown to the current crisis due to these storms, sets our nation apart from any other nation. Our nation does not have a perfect history by any means, but we strive for improvement. Our nation is a democracy where people have the right to live as they desire. Our nation is a new nation as history goes. However, through our courage, strength, and a strong determination, America will continue to prosper and lead the way for all nations into the future.

Activity Options

1. Observe photographs of the damage caused by recent hurricanes.

2. Watch video of hurricane victims in New Orleans.

3. List the characteristics of a category-four or-five hurricane.

4. Record the changes in the environment in Mississippi where Hurricane Katrina struck.

5. Design a map that indicates where hurricanes struck in 2004 and 2005.

6. Record the health hazards that Hurricane Katrina caused in New Orleans.

Experience U.S. History! • Rickey Millwood
Kagan Publishing • 1 (800) 933-2667 • www.KaganOnline.com

Notes

Kagan
It's All About Engagement!

Kagan is the world leader in creating active engagement in the classroom. Learn how to engage your students and you will boost achievement, prevent discipline problems, and make learning more fun and meaningful. Come join Kagan for a workshop or call Kagan to **set up a workshop for your school or district**. Experience the power of a Kagan workshop.

Experience the engagement!

SPECIALIZING IN:

- ★ **Cooperative Learning**
- ★ **Win-Win Discipline**
- ★ **Brain-Friendly Teaching**
- ★ **Multiple Intelligences**
- ★ **Thinking Skills**
- ★ **Kagan Coaching**

KAGAN PROFESSIONAL DEVELOPMENT

www.KaganOnline.com ★ 1(800) 266-7576

Kagan

It's All About Engagement!

**Kagan is your source
for active engagement in the classroom.**

Check out Kagan's line of books, SmartCards, software, electronics, and hands-on learning resources—all designed to boost engagement in your classroom.

Books

SmartCards

Software

Learning Chips

Spinners

Learning Cubes

KAGAN PUBLISHING

www.KaganOnline.com ★ 1(800) 933-2667